YOUNG, GIFTED & GRINDING:

How to Turn Sidewalk Sales into Passive Income & Get Paid for Life

BY BUSINESSMAN CEDRIC

DISCLAIMER

The advice contained in this material might not be suitable for everyone. The authors designed the information to present their opinion about the subject matter. The reader must carefully investigate all aspects of any business decision before committing to him or herself. The authors obtained the information contained herein from sources they believe to be reliable and from their own personal experiences, but they neither imply nor intend any guarantee of accuracy. The authors are not in the business of giving legal, accounting, or any other type of professional advice. Should the reader need such advice, he or she must seek services from a competent professional. The authors particularly disclaims any liability, loss, or risk taken by individuals who directly or indirectly act on the information contained herein. The authors believe the advice presented here is sound, but readers cannot hold them responsible for either the actions they take, or the risk taken by individuals who directly or indirectly act on the information contained herein.

Published by 1Brick Publishing
Printed in the United States
Copyright © 2025 by Cedric Duncan
ISBN 979-8898560096

DEDICATION

To my grandmother, who looked me in my eyes before she passed and said, "Boy, you gonna be on that stage" and "You the man of the house now." Your belief in me lit a fire that will never go out.

To my mother, who taught me the meaning of hustle through her own example. Watching you work so hard is what drove me to find a way to ease your burden. Every dollar I make is a testament to your strength.

To everyone who's ever been told their dreams are too big or their circumstances are too limiting—this book proves that with God, hustle, and heart, nothing is impossible.

Without God, I'm nothing.

DEDICATION REQUEST

Please pass this book to a young entrepreneur who's ready to break generational curses and build wealth that lasts—it's the guide I wish I had when I started my journey.

TABLE OF CONTENTS

FOREWORD

Some meetings are coincidences. Others are divine appointments.

When I first met Cedric in that parking lot at Nehemiah Davis's food giveaway, I wasn't even supposed to be there. I had another event I was hosting, but something pulled me to show up anyway—dressed in my suit, looking out of place among the crowd. Now I understand why. God needed me to meet this young man.

I noticed him immediately—17 years old, selling hats with a confidence and purpose that stood out. As we talked, I saw something in him that took me right back to my own beginnings. At 8 years old, I was packing grocery bags at the local supermarket, trying to help my mother keep food on the table and a roof over our heads. I know intimately the weight of watching your mother do her absolute best and still struggle. But I also know the indescribable joy of being able to ease some of that burden through your own efforts.

What struck me most wasn't just Cedric's hustle—it was his vision. While many young men his age are focused solely on the present, Cedric was already talking about real estate, passive income, and building a legacy. He wasn't just selling hats; he was funding his future. He wasn't just making money; he was breaking generational curses.

The parallels between our journeys are almost eerie. His mother and my mother had us at the same age. We both started hustling young out of necessity, not choice. We both chose the legal path when illegal opportunities were right in front of us. We share the same drive, the same entrepreneurial spirit, the same desire to create something that outlasts us.

But Cedric has something at 17 that I didn't have—guidance. When I was coming up, I had to learn these lessons through trial and error, sometimes at great cost. The blueprint you're holding in your hands is the resource I wish someone had given me at his age. It would have accelerated my journey and helped me avoid countless pitfalls.

This book isn't just theory. It's not written by someone who studied business in a classroom but never sold a product on the street. It's written by someone who has lived it—who continues to live it—who makes $800 a day through sheer hustle, charisma, and strategy. It's written by someone who understands that the skills learned on the streets, when channeled properly, can build empires.

What makes Cedric special isn't just his business acumen, though that's impressive. It's his wisdom beyond his years. It's his understanding that true success isn't measured by what you accumulate, but by what you create, who you become, and who you lift as you climb.

In a world that often tells young people from our communities that their options are limited, Cedric stands as living proof that entrepreneurship is a viable path to freedom. His story challenges the narrative that success requires either exceptional luck or exceptional privilege. It demonstrates that with hustle, heart, and the right game plan, you can create opportunities where others see none.

I believe that Cedric's potential is limitless. With the right guidance, support, and continued determination, there's no goal he can't achieve. I'm honored to play a small role in his journey, and I'm excited for you to learn from his experiences and insights.

Whether you're a teenager looking for your first dollar, an adult trying to escape the paycheck-to-paycheck cycle, or someone who simply appreciates the raw wisdom that comes from real-life experience, this book has something valuable to offer you.

Read it. Apply it. Share it. And remember that the streets may have taught us how to hustle, but this book will teach you how to own the block.

Ash Cash Exantus
Bestselling Author, Financial Educator, and Entrepreneur

INTRODUCTION

FROM RENT TO RICHES

I was seventeen when I realized I had two choices: make excuses or make money.

My mom's car had broken down, which meant she couldn't drive for Uber—our main source of income. We were already three months behind on rent. I remember watching her cry in her room, feeling helpless as the bills piled up. Not because she didn't work hard (my mother has always been the hardest worker I know), but because in our neighborhood, hard work and fair pay rarely went hand-in-hand.

I remember the feeling that hit my chest that night—not just worry, but a fire. I knew I had to act. I had to make something shake, or we were going to get put out. While some of my friends were choosing illegal hustles, I decided to create a different path.

I took what little money I had and bought some hats from Little Giants. The first day I went out selling, I came home with $140. My mom couldn't believe it. The next day, I made $200. Within a week of blood, sweat, and tears, I had made enough to cover our three months of back rent—about $3,000. That's when everything changed.

When I placed that money in my mother's hands, something shifted inside me. It wasn't just about paying the rent. I had discovered something many adults never find: the power to create value out of thin air.

Now I make at least $800 a day selling hats and chains with positive messages. But the road here wasn't easy. I've faced my share of dangerous situations that made me choose this path. I used to sell weed and got caught up in a fight that ended with people shooting at the car I was in. Two bullets hit my door but didn't go through. That's when I knew God was protecting me, and I put "Without God I'm Nothing" on my hats.

In the streets where I'm from, there are two paths to quick cash, but only one leads to freedom. I chose the legal route not just because it's right, but because it's sustainable. You can really lose your life chasing a quick illegal buck. I'd rather make money legally, even if it takes more work.

This book isn't about getting rich quick. There's no secret formula or shortcut to success. What you'll find in these pages is something much more valuable: a blueprint for turning your hustle into a legacy.

Whether you're a teenager trying to help your family make ends meet or an adult trapped in the paycheck-to-paycheck cycle, this book is for you. I'll show you how to:

- Start exactly where you are with whatever you have
- Sell with confidence and purpose—even when you're scared
- Build a team that multiplies your efforts and income
- Transform your hard-earned money into passive income through investments like vending machines, real estate, and more
- Break generational curses and create wealth that lasts

When my grandmother passed in July 2023, she looked me in my eyes and said, "Boy, you gonna be on that stage," and "You the man of the house now." Nobody in my family has ever been a millionaire or financially free. I have to break those generational curses.

Some days I want to quit. I'll be honest—90% of what I do, I don't want to do. But my why is so strong that I push through anyway. That's what separates real hustlers from people who just talk about it. A real hustler goes out there even when it's difficult, even when they're not making it. They still go out there and get it all.

The streets taught me how to hustle, but vision taught me how to build. Now, it's your turn.

Let's get to work.

—*Businessman Cedric*

CHAPTER 1

YOUNG, GIFTED & FOCUSED

THE ADVANTAGE OF STARTING EARLY

Most people think being young is a disadvantage in business. They'll tell you that you need experience, connections, or a college degree before you can start making real money.

They're wrong.

Being young is actually your greatest asset—if you know how to use it. When I walk up to someone with my hats, being 17 years old isn't something I hide or apologize for. It's the first thing I tell them: "Hey, how you doing today? I'm sorry to bother you, gonna be real quick. My name is Cedric. I'm a 17-year-old entrepreneur."

Why? Because people respect hustle at any age, but they're especially impressed by it when you're young. While your friends are playing video games or hanging out, you're out building something real. That stands out. That creates opportunity.

But it's not just about how others see you—it's about how starting early gives you room to fail, learn, and grow. I've been selling since I was in high school, and I've already learned lessons that some people don't figure out until they're 40. By the time I'm 25, I'll have almost a decade of business experience. Think about that advantage.

SURVIVAL VS. STRATEGY: THE MINDSET DIFFERENCE

There are two types of hustlers in this world:

1. **Survival Hustlers** wake up thinking, "How am I going to eat today?" They're focused on the next meal, the next bill, the next problem. They work hard but never get ahead because they're always putting out fires instead of building something that lasts.
2. **Strategic Hustlers** wake up thinking, "How am I going to build today?" They might start with the same problems and the same hustle, but they're always looking beyond the immediate paycheck to the bigger picture.

I started as a survival hustler. When my mom's car broke down and we were three months behind on rent, I wasn't thinking about building a brand or investing in real estate. I was thinking about keeping a roof over our heads. That urgent need gave me the motivation to start—but if I had stayed in that survival mindset, I would have stopped once the rent was paid.

The turning point came when I realized I could do more than just survive—I could thrive. Instead of seeing each sale as just $15 in my pocket, I started seeing it as a building block for something bigger.

That shift from survival to strategy is what separates those who hustle temporarily from those who build wealth permanently.

LEGAL HUSTLE VS. STREET HUSTLE

Let me be real with you: Where I'm from, there are plenty of ways to make fast money—but most of them end with you in jail, in the hospital, or in the ground.

I know because I've been there. I used to sell weed and got caught up in dangerous situations. One day, after an argument at school with some older guys, we were supposed to fight it out by the lake. They showed up 30 deep, all wearing black. During the fight, I could feel the guy clutching his gun. When we tried to leave, they shot at our car four times. Two bullets hit my door but didn't go through.

That was God protecting me. That was my wake-up call.

The street hustle might look attractive when you see guys flashing money, wearing expensive clothes, and driving nice cars. But what you don't see is the constant looking over your shoulder, the friends who get locked up or worse, and the families torn apart.

The legal hustle isn't always as fast. It takes more creativity, more persistence, and sometimes more patience. But here's what it gives you that the street hustle never can: freedom.

- Freedom to walk down the street without worrying about who's watching
- Freedom to build something you can talk about proudly with anyone
- Freedom to plan for the future instead of just surviving the present
- Freedom to sleep peacefully at night knowing tomorrow is coming

My hat business makes me $800 a day now—sometimes more. That's good money in any neighborhood. But more importantly, it's clean money. Money that builds instead of destroys. Money that opens doors instead of closing them.

FOCUS: YOUR SUPERPOWER

Young, gifted, and grinding isn't just a catchy phrase—it's a mindset. And the most important part of that mindset is focus.

Focus means knowing what you want and eliminating everything that doesn't help you get there. For me, that meant dropping out of high school in 11th grade. Now, I'm not telling everyone to drop out—education is valuable. But I knew my path, and I was already making $3,000-$4,000 a week selling hats.

When I told my teacher I was going to start hustling, she shook her head. People will always doubt your vision when they can't see what you see. That's why focus is so important—it helps you tune out the doubters and stay locked on your goals.

Here's how I stay focused every day:

1. **I start with prayer.** Every morning, I thank God for both the good times and the bad times. I put my day in His hands and ask for guidance, not for money.

2. **I remind myself of my why.** My grandmother told me before she passed in 2023, "Boy, you gonna be on that stage," and "You're the man of the house now." Nobody in my family has ever been a millionaire or financially free. I have to break those generational curses.

3. **I embrace the grind.** I'll be honest—90% of what I do, I don't want to do. But I do it anyway because I know where it's taking me. That's what separates real hustlers from people who just talk.

4. **I visualize the end goal.** I've been in rooms with people wearing quarter-million-dollar watches, saying that's "something slight." In their world, that's normal. I want to create that normal for myself and my family.

Focus doesn't mean never having bad days. I have plenty of days when I want to quit, when negative thoughts creep in. But focus means pushing through those days anyway, knowing that each step brings me closer to my goals.

YOUR GIFT IS ALREADY INSIDE YOU

Everyone is gifted at something. Some people can talk to anyone. Others are great with numbers. Some can fix things, build things, or create things that others can't.

Your gift might not be obvious at first. It might be hidden under layers of doubt, fear, or simply not knowing what you're good at yet. But I promise you—it's there.

My gift is connecting with people. I can walk up to a stranger and make them feel comfortable. I can read their energy and adjust my approach. I can make them laugh and lower their guard. That gift isn't something I learned in school—it's something I discovered by putting myself out there and trying.

You might not know what your gift is yet, but here's how to find it:

1. **Try different things.** I started selling five-dollar T-shirts from Five Below for $25 before I found my sweet spot with hats.
2. **Pay attention to what comes naturally.** What do people compliment you on? What do you do better than most people around you?
3. **Notice what energizes you.** When you're using your gift, time flies. It doesn't feel like work.

Once you find your gift, focus on developing it. Read books about it. Find mentors who excel at it. Practice it daily.

Remember: Being young and gifted isn't enough—you also need to be focused. Without focus, your gift is just potential. With focus, it becomes your superpower.

ACTION STEPS:

1. **Identify Your Starting Point**: Write down exactly where you are right now—your skills, resources, and opportunities. Don't focus on what you lack. Focus on what you have.

2. **Clarify Your Why**: What's driving you? Is it helping your family? Breaking generational curses? Creating freedom for yourself? Write it down and keep it somewhere you'll see it daily.

3. **Choose Your Hustle**: What legal skills or products could you sell right now? Make a list of three possible hustles based on what's already available to you.

4. **Set a 30-Day Goal**: What specific outcome do you want to achieve in the next month? Make it challenging but achievable.

5. **Find Your Daily Discipline**: What one action can you commit to doing every single day that will move you toward your goal?

Remember, the difference between those who talk about success and those who achieve it isn't age, education, or connections—it's action. Being young and gifted means nothing without being focused enough to take that first step, and the thousand steps after it.

Now stop reading and start doing.

CHAPTER 2

CONFIDENCE IS CURRENCY

THE REAL MONEY MAKER

Let me tell you a secret that most people never figure out: In sales, your product matters—but your confidence matters more.

I sell hats for $15 that probably cost me a few dollars. Why do people buy them? Not because they desperately need another hat. They buy because of the confidence I bring to that interaction. The energy. The belief. The connection.

When I approach someone, I'm not just selling a hat—I'm selling myself. I'm selling the idea that supporting me is better than supporting something negative. I'm selling the vision of what their purchase can help create.

Confidence is the real currency in this game. It's what turns a simple product into a movement. It's what makes people stop, listen, and reach for their wallets.

And here's the best part: Unlike money, confidence is something you can create out of thin air. You don't need to be born with it. You don't need to wait for someone to give it to you. You just need to understand how it works and practice it daily.

ENERGY, EYE CONTACT, AND PRESENCE

When I walk up to someone, before I even open my mouth, I've already started selling. How? Through my energy, eye contact, and presence.

Energy is how you carry yourself. It's the vibe you give off. People can feel whether you're excited, bored, desperate, or confident. I make sure my energy says, "I believe in what I'm doing. I'm here to offer value, not beg for money."

Even on days when I don't feel like hustling—and trust me, that's about 90% of days—I still bring that positive energy. Why? Because energy is contagious. If I approach someone with low, defeated energy, why would they get excited about what I'm selling?

Eye contact is your first connection. When I look someone in the eye, I'm saying, "I see you as a person, not just a potential customer." Eye contact builds trust. It shows confidence. It demands attention.

Many people are afraid to make eye contact because they're afraid of rejection. But here's the thing: the rejection is coming either way if that's what the person decides. Avoiding eye contact just makes the rejection more likely.

Presence means being fully there in the moment. Not checking your phone. Not looking around for the next customer. Not rushing through your pitch because you've said it a hundred times already.

When I'm talking to someone, I give them my full presence. I listen to their objections. I respond to their energy. I adjust my approach based on what I'm feeling from them.

This combination—energy, eye contact, and presence—creates an immediate impression that gets people to stop and listen instead of walking by.

THE WALK-UP METHOD: BREAKING FEAR AND OWNING YOUR SPACE

The hardest part of sales is the approach. That first step when you walk up to a complete stranger and interrupt their day is where most people freeze up. I call what I do the "Walk-Up Method," and it's about breaking through that fear and owning your space in any environment.

Here's how it works:

1. **Choose your target wisely.** Not everyone is a potential customer. I look for people who aren't in a rush, who have a positive expression, or who make eye contact with me first. Reading people is key.
2. **Approach with purpose.** Walk directly toward them with confidence. No hesitation. No circling around. Direct movement shows confidence.
3. **Start with respect.** My opening line is always: "Hey, how you doing today? I'm sorry to bother you, gonna be real quick."

This acknowledges that I'm interrupting them but promises I won't waste their time.

4. **Introduce yourself with pride.** "My name is Cedric. I'm a 17-year-old entrepreneur." I state my age immediately because it's part of my story. It makes people curious.

5. **Make it about more than the product.** "These money hats, they say, 'Without God, I'm nothing.' That's because I'm out here trying to show you that you could sling instead of slinging drugs."

6. **Share your bigger goal.** "I'm also out here trying to fund my real estate business."

7. **Build social proof.** "Most people been buying stuff. They say they'd rather see me selling hope instead of selling dope. Don't you agree?"

8. **Make the ask simple.** "It's just $15, that's like showing bubble gum. Can you do it from the heart and not your pockets?"

9. **Close without pressure.** Whether they say yes or no, I stay positive. If they're rude, I just say, "God bless you. See you around. Stay positive."

This method works because it breaks through the awkwardness that stops most people from approaching strangers. Once you've done it a few times, the fear starts to fade.

STAYING CONFIDENT WHEN PEOPLE SAY "NO"

Here's something that took me a while to learn: Rejection isn't personal. It's just part of the process.

When someone says "no" to me, I don't take it as a failure. I take it as one step closer to the next "yes." Sales is a numbers game. If I approach 20 people and 15 say no, that might sound bad at first. But if 5 say yes at $15 each, that's $75 for a few minutes of work.

I remember when I first started out, every "no" felt like a punch to the gut. It made me question whether I should even be doing this. But then I had a realization that changed everything for me: Even Jesus didn't convince everybody.

Think about it—if the son of God himself couldn't get everyone to believe in him, who am I to think I should have a 100% close rate? It's the same with any product. Tesla doesn't sell to everyone. Nike doesn't sell to everyone. No business has a perfect conversion rate.

Once I understood that, rejection lost its power over me. Now, when someone says "no" or ignores me or even gets a little rude, I just smile and say, "God bless you. Stay positive." And I move on to the next person with the same energy and confidence.

Sometimes, that positive response to rejection even turns things around. I've had people who were mean to me turn back around and give me $100, apologizing for being disrespectful. Why? Because my energy stayed positive even when theirs didn't.

Remember: Confidence isn't the absence of rejection—it's the ability to maintain your energy despite it.

CONFIDENCE TRICKS: TURNING WEAKNESSES INTO STRENGTHS

One of the most powerful ways to build confidence is to stop hiding your weaknesses and start using them as strengths. Let me give you some examples of how I do this:

Age: Most young sellers try to act older than they are. I do the opposite. I immediately tell people I'm 17 because it makes me stand out. It shows I'm doing something different at a young age.

Background: I don't hide the fact that I come from a neighborhood where selling drugs is common. Instead, I use it: "They'd rather see me selling hope instead of selling dope."

Rejection: When I sense someone might say no, I sometimes say, "Can you say yes like my mom, and don't say no like my dad?" or "Don't break my heart like my last girlfriend did." This turns potential rejection into a moment of connection and humor.

Lack of experience: Instead of pretending I know everything, I position myself as hungry to learn: "I don't know nothing. I'm just a sponge. I just want game."

These "tricks" work because they're authentic. I'm not making things up—I'm just framing my real situation in a way that connects rather than creates distance.

THE PSYCHOLOGY OF SALES: 90% MENTAL, 10% PHYSICAL

Sales isn't primarily about the physical act of exchanging products for money. It's about the mental game happening between your ears and in the mind of your customer.

I've studied sales psychology by reading books and watching people like "Funny Salesman." What I've learned is that for every objection, there's a counter that can keep the conversation going.

If someone says, "I'm too busy right now, I'm in a rush," I say, "Can I join the race?" This creates a moment of surprise that often leads to a smile, which opens the door to more conversation.

If someone asks, "Why do you need the money?" that's not a "no"— that's an objection. And objections mean they're interested enough to engage. They're giving you something to talk about.

Understanding this psychology helps me stay confident because I know that what looks like rejection is often just the start of a negotiation. You'll get probably 10 nos, 5 nos first, and after them 10 nos, you're just gonna get straight yeses.

It's really 90% mental, 10% physical. Like a walk in the park, though, you got to talk to yourself while you're out there.

BUILDING CONFIDENCE THROUGH PRACTICE

Confidence isn't something you're born with—it's something you build through practice. Here's how I built mine:

1. **Start small.** When I first began approaching strangers, I was nervous too. I started with people who seemed more approachable, like older women who reminded me of my grandmother.
2. **Set small goals.** At first, my goal wasn't to make $800 a day. It was just to approach five people and make one sale. Small wins build confidence.
3. **Use rejection as training.** Every time someone says no, I ask myself why. What could I have done differently? Was it my approach, my pitch, or just not the right person? This turns rejection into a learning opportunity.
4. **Practice with friends.** I tell my friends, "Ask me for a piece of candy." When they do, I say no. Then I tell them to ask my mom. She asks why they want candy. I explain that her question is an objection—it shows interest. This helps me understand sales dynamics.
5. **Watch other successful salespeople.** I study how they move, how they talk, how they handle objections. Success leaves clues.
6. **Celebrate wins.** Every sale, no matter how small, is proof that I can do this. I take a moment to appreciate each one.

Remember, the goal isn't to become someone else. It's to become the most confident version of yourself. Your unique energy, your story, your way of connecting with people—that's what will set you apart.

ACTION STEPS:

1. **Record Your Pitch:** Use your phone to record yourself giving your sales pitch. Watch it back. How's your energy? Your eye contact? Your confidence? Make notes on what to improve.

2. **The Five Approach Challenge:** Go to a public place and challenge yourself to approach five strangers with your product or idea. Focus on maintaining confidence through all five, regardless of the outcome.

3. **Create Your Response Arsenal:** Write down the five most common objections you hear and create a positive, engaging response to each one.

4. **Mirror Practice:** Spend five minutes each morning looking in the mirror and practicing your pitch with full eye contact and energy.

5. **Confidence Journal:** At the end of each day, write down one moment when you showed confidence and one situation where you could have been more confident. Track your progress over time.

Remember, confidence isn't just how you feel—it's how you act despite how you feel. It's showing up with energy and purpose even on days when you'd rather stay home. It's approaching the next person with the same enthusiasm after you've just been rejected.

And most importantly, confidence is a skill—not a personality trait. Anyone can develop it with practice and the right mindset.

Confidence truly is currency. Start investing in yourself today.

CHAPTER 3

THE SIDEWALK SALES SYSTEM

CHOOSING A PRODUCT WITH PURPOSE

When most people think about starting a business, they overthink it. They spend months researching markets, analyzing competitors, and trying to find the perfect product. Meanwhile, opportunities pass them by.

I took a different approach. I needed to make money fast when my mom was three months behind on rent. I didn't have time for perfect—I needed something I could start with immediately.

That's how I ended up selling hats with "Without God I'm Nothing" on them. It wasn't because market research told me religious hats would sell well. It was because:

1. **I could afford to get started.** Hats have a low entry cost compared to many other products.
2. **The message meant something to me.** After getting shot at and seeing how God protected me, "Without

God I'm Nothing" wasn't just a catchy phrase—it was my truth.

3. **The product was portable.** I could carry my inventory with me anywhere without needing a car or storage space.

4. **People already buy hats.** I didn't have to create demand for a new type of product.

Before the hats, I tried selling T-shirts from Five Below. I'd buy them for $5 and sell them for $25. When they had sayings like "Sarcasm Served Daily," I'd use that in my pitch: "I put 'Sarcasm Served Daily' because that's how people been treating me out here." It made people laugh and connect with me.

The lesson? Start with what you can afford, what you believe in, and what you can easily sell. Your first product doesn't need to be your forever product—it just needs to get you in the game.

UNDERSTANDING WHAT PEOPLE WANT

People don't buy products—they buy value, messages, and vibes.

Value isn't just about the price tag. It's about what your product means to the person buying it. When someone buys one of my hats, they're not just getting something to wear. They're supporting a young entrepreneur instead of someone selling drugs. They're part of my journey to break generational curses. They're making a statement about their own faith.

That's why I say in my pitch: "Most people been buying stuff. They say they'd rather see me selling hope instead of selling dope. Don't you agree?" This isn't just a line—it's showing the real value beyond the physical product.

Message is what your product communicates. My hats say "Without God I'm Nothing" because that message resonates with many people in my community. It's authentic to my story and connects with others who share similar values.

Your message should be something you believe in. People can tell when you're just saying things to make a sale versus when you're sharing something real.

Vibe is the feeling people get when they interact with you and your product. Are you excited? Passionate? Genuine? The energy you bring to your hustle impacts how people respond to it.

I make sure my vibe is always positive, even when people say no. I stay respectful and wish them well: "God bless you. See you around. Stay positive." This vibe has actually turned situations around, with people who initially rejected me coming back to make a purchase or even give me more than I asked for.

Understanding these three elements—value, message, and vibe—will help you choose products that connect with people, not just products that look good or seem trendy.

THE BASICS OF PRODUCT PRESENTATION

While I usually sell hand-to-hand, I've learned a lot about how to present products effectively. Whether you have a physical table or are carrying your inventory, presentation matters.

Visibility

People need to see what you're selling. If you have a table, your products should be neatly arranged and visible from different angles. If you're mobile like me, you need to be able to show your product quickly and clearly.

I carry my hats in a way that makes the message visible. When I approach someone, I make sure they can immediately see the quality and design.

Cleanliness

Nothing turns customers away faster than dirty or damaged products. Keep your inventory clean and in good condition. This shows respect for both your products and your customers.

For my hats, I make sure they're free from dust, fingerprints, or any damage. When people see that I take care of my products, they're more likely to value them.

Organization

Even if you only sell one type of product, organization matters. Having different colors organized logically makes it easier for customers to find what they want.

I sort my hats by color—black, blue, pink. When someone shows interest, I can quickly show them the options without fumbling around.

Signage

If you have a table or fixed location, clear signage helps communicate your message even when you're not actively pitching. Your sign should answer basic questions: What is this? How much does it cost? Why should I care?

While I don't always use signs since I'm mobile, I've noticed that when I display my "Without God I'm Nothing" message prominently, it sometimes starts conversations without me having to initiate.

LOCATION, LOCATION, LOCATION

Where you sell is almost as important as what you sell. The right location puts you in front of people who are ready to buy.

I look for:

High-Traffic Areas: Places where lots of people naturally walk by. Grocery store parking lots, mall entrances, and busy street corners work well. More people means more potential customers.

The Right Timing: I pay attention to when people get paid. Selling outside a grocery store on the first of the month, when people receive government benefits, can lead to better sales than choosing a random day.

Appropriate Settings: Some products sell better in certain environments. My "Without God I'm Nothing" hats connect well with church crowds or community events. Think about where your ideal customers already gather.

Legal Spots: Getting kicked out or dealing with security wastes time and creates negative energy. I make sure I'm in places where I'm allowed to sell, or at least where no one will bother me.

Safety First: No sale is worth putting yourself in danger. I avoid areas known for crime or violence. Your physical safety is more important than any potential profit.

The perfect location combines all these factors. For me, busy retail parking lots on weekends or at the beginning of the month have proven most successful.

CEDRIC'S STREET SALES SCRIPT & STRATEGIES

I promised to break down my exact sales approach, so here it is— the full script I use when approaching someone new:

"Hey, how you doing today? I'm sorry to bother you, gonna be real quick. My name is Cedric. I'm a 17-year-old entrepreneur. These money hats, they say 'Without God I'm Nothing.' That's because I'm out here trying to show you that you could sling instead of slinging drugs. I'm also out here trying to fund my real estate business. Most people been buying stuff. They say they'd rather see me selling hope instead of selling dope. Don't you agree? It's just $15, that's like showing bubble gum. Can you do it from the heart and not your pockets?"

Let's break down why this works:

1. **Respectful Opening:** "I'm sorry to bother you" acknowledges that I'm interrupting their day and shows respect for their time.
2. **Personal Introduction:** I immediately share my name and age, making the interaction personal and highlighting my youth as an advantage.
3. **Product Description:** I clearly state what I'm selling and the message it represents.
4. **Purpose Beyond Product:** I explain that this isn't just about selling hats—it's about choosing a positive path and building toward bigger goals like real estate.
5. **Social Proof:** "Most people been buying" suggests others have already validated this purchase.
6. **Value Comparison:** "They'd rather see me selling hope instead of selling dope" frames the purchase as supporting something positive.
7. **Agreement Question:** "Don't you agree?" is designed to get a "yes" that sets up the actual purchase.
8. **Price Minimization:** "It's just $15, that's like showing bubble gum" makes the price seem small compared to its impact.
9. **Heart Appeal:** "Can you do it from the heart and not your pockets?" frames the purchase as an act of kindness rather than a financial decision.

This script has been refined through hundreds of interactions. It addresses common objections before they're raised and creates an emotional connection that goes beyond the product itself.

HANDLING OBJECTIONS ON THE STREET

In sales, objections are just part of the conversation. Here's how I handle the most common ones:

"I don't have any cash right now."

Response: "No problem! I take Cash App, Venmo, or even credit cards." (Always have multiple payment options ready)

"I'm in a rush."

Response: "Can I join the race?" (This often gets a laugh and opens the door to continue talking)

"I already have too many hats."

Response: "This one's different though—it's not just a hat, it's supporting a young entrepreneur's dream. Plus, it looks better than the ones you already have!" (Said with a smile)

"Why should I buy this?"

Response: "Great question! This isn't just about the hat. When you buy this, you're helping me build my real estate business and showing other young people there's a better path than selling drugs. Plus, it's a quality hat with a message that reminds us who's really in control."

"I need to think about it."

Response: "I respect that. What specifically do you need to think about? Maybe I can help address those concerns right now."

The key to handling objections is to never take them personally and to always respond with respect. Some people will still say no, and that's okay. Thank them for their time and move on with the same positive energy.

CLOSING THE SALE

The moment of asking for the money is where many new hustlers freeze up. Here's how I make it natural and comfortable:

1. **Assume the sale.** After my pitch, I often just hold out the hat as if the person has already decided to buy it. This positive assumption makes it easier for them to say yes.
2. **Make paying easy.** I'm ready to accept multiple forms of payment. The easier you make it to pay, the more likely people are to follow through.
3. **Use humor to ease tension.** Sometimes I'll say something like "Don't break my heart like my last girlfriend did" when asking for the purchase. This lightens the mood and makes saying no feel more awkward than saying yes.
4. **Close with gratitude.** When someone buys from me, I express genuine appreciation. "Thank you so much for supporting me. This really helps me get closer to my goals."
5. **Add value after the purchase.** I might offer a quick prayer or word of encouragement after someone buys.

This makes them feel good about their purchase and more likely to remember me.

LEARNING FROM EVERY INTERACTION

Every person you approach is an opportunity to learn, whether they buy or not. Here's what I pay attention to:

1. **What worked?** Notice which parts of your pitch got positive reactions—a nod, a smile, leaning in closer.
2. **What didn't work?** Be honest about moments that created hesitation or confusion.
3. **Who responded best?** Start recognizing patterns in the types of people who are most receptive to your product and approach.
4. **What objections came up?** Write down new objections you haven't heard before and develop responses for next time.

When I started, I kept a small notebook where I'd write down objections and my responses to them. This helped me refine my approach over time. Sales is a skill, and like any skill, it improves with deliberate practice and reflection.

Remember—my first day selling, I made $140. Now I consistently make $800 or more per day. That improvement didn't happen by accident. It came from paying attention, learning from each interaction, and constantly refining my approach.

ACTION STEPS:

1. **Product Selection Exercise:** List three products you could start selling tomorrow based on what you already have access to or can afford to purchase. For each product, write down why someone would want it beyond its basic function.

2. **Script Development:** Write your own sales script following the structure I outlined. Practice it until it feels natural, not rehearsed.

3. **Location Scouting:** Identify three potential selling locations in your area. Visit each one at different times to observe foot traffic and the types of people present.

4. **Objection Collection:** After your first day selling, write down every objection you received. Create a response for each one before going out again.

5. **Sales Journal:** Keep track of your daily sales, noting what worked well and what could be improved. Look for patterns that can help you refine your approach.

The sidewalk sales system isn't complicated, but it does require consistency and a willingness to learn. Start with what you have, where you are, and keep refining your approach based on real-world feedback.

Remember: The streets are the best business school you'll ever attend. Every interaction teaches you something valuable if you're paying attention.

CHAPTER 4

DIGITAL DOLLARS

TAKING YOUR HUSTLE ONLINE

The same hustle that works on sidewalks can work on screens.

When I first started selling hats, I was focused on face-to-face interactions because that's what I knew. But being around Neo, Meet, Wolf, and Ash showed me something important: the power of social media can multiply your reach beyond what's physically possible.

Think about it—on a good day, I might interact with 50-100 people in person. But a single post on Instagram can reach thousands. A viral video can reach millions. The digital world doesn't have the same physical limitations as the streets.

But here's what most people miss: the principles that make you successful on the sidewalk are the same ones that make you successful online. You still need confidence. You still need to connect with people. You still need to offer value beyond just your product.

The difference is scale. When I sell a hat to someone in a parking lot, that's one sale. But when I build a following online, I create opportunities for hundreds or thousands of sales—while I sleep, while I'm at another event, or while I'm working on building my next venture.

This chapter isn't about abandoning the streets for the screens. It's about using both to create something bigger than either could produce alone.

THE ONLINE ADVANTAGE

Taking your hustle online has several advantages over strictly in-person sales:

24/7 Availability: Your online store never closes. People can discover and buy your products at 3 AM while you're sleeping.

Unlimited Geographical Reach: Instead of being limited to your local area, you can sell to people across the country or even internationally.

Storytelling Opportunities: Social media gives you space to share your journey, your why, and the impact your business is making—all of which helps people connect with you beyond just your products.

Data and Analytics: Online platforms give you insights about who's interested in your products, what they're clicking on, and how they found you. This helps you make smarter decisions.

Lower Barrier to Purchase: Some people who would never stop on the street will happily buy online where there's less social pressure.

Here's a perfect example from my own experience: when Ash posted about me on Instagram, I immediately gained followers and started getting more attention. Those followers became potential customers, and some of those potential customers became actual buyers. All from a single post.

That's the power of digital dollars—one moment of exposure can create ongoing opportunities.

SETTING UP YOUR DIGITAL STOREFRONT

You don't need to be a tech genius to start selling online. Here are the basics you need to get started:

Instagram Shop

Instagram is where many of my customers already spend time, making it the perfect place to start selling. To set up an Instagram Shop:

1. **Convert to a Business Account:** This gives you access to insights about your followers and allows you to create a shop.
2. **Connect to Facebook:** Your Instagram Shop will be linked to a Facebook Page, so you'll need to create one if you don't have one already.
3. **Upload Your Catalog:** Add your products with clear photos, descriptions, and prices.
4. **Set Up Checkout:** Make it easy for customers to buy directly through the app.

The best part about Instagram is that it combines your store with your content, allowing people to see both your products and your story in one place.

Payment Options

To make sales easy, set up multiple payment methods:

Cash App: Quick and easy for both you and your customers. Just create an account with a unique username that's easy to remember.

Venmo: Similar to Cash App but with different users. Having both options widens your potential customer base.

Square: Allows you to accept credit cards in person or online. You can get a free card reader that connects to your phone.

PayPal: Good for online transactions, especially if you're selling to people internationally.

Having multiple payment options eliminates "I don't have cash" as an objection and makes it easier for people to support you.

Shopify Basics

For a more professional online store, Shopify is worth the investment:

1. **Choose a Plan:** Start with the basic plan until your sales justify an upgrade.
2. **Select a Theme:** Pick a clean, simple design that showcases your products.

3. **Add Your Products:** Upload high-quality photos and write descriptions that tell the story behind each item.
4. **Set Up Shipping:** Decide how much to charge for shipping and which carriers you'll use.
5. **Connect Payment Processors:** Link your store to payment methods like Stripe, PayPal, and Shop Pay.

Shopify gives you more control and looks more professional than selling solely through social media, but it does come with monthly costs. Start with Instagram and expand to Shopify once you have consistent sales.

CREATING CONTENT THAT SELLS

On social media, your content is your pitch. Instead of approaching people directly, you're creating content that draws them to you. Here's how to make it effective:

Show, Don't Just Tell

Don't just post product photos. Show your hustle in action:

- Record videos of yourself selling on the street
- Capture genuine customer reactions
- Document your journey from where you started to where you are now

People connect with stories more than products. Let them see the real person behind the brand.

Keep It Short and Engaging

Attention spans are short online. Your content should:

- Get to the point quickly
- Start with something attention-grabbing
- Be authentic to who you are
- Include a clear call to action

The same energy that makes people stop on the street needs to come through in your videos and posts.

Use the Right Hashtags

Hashtags help people discover your content. Research which ones are most relevant to your products and audience. For example, with my hats, I might use:

- #FaithBasedClothing
- #StreetEntrepreneur
- #YoungHustler
- #WithoutGodImNothing
- #BlackOwnedBusiness

Mix popular hashtags with more specific ones to increase your chances of being discovered.

Consistency Matters

Post regularly to stay in people's feeds and minds. Even if it's just a quick update or a motivational quote, consistent content keeps your audience engaged.

I recommend planning your content in advance. Set aside time each week to create several posts that you can spread throughout the week.

BUILDING YOUR DIGITAL COMMUNITY

Online success isn't just about making one-time sales—it's about building a community of supporters who come back again and again. Here's how:

Engage Authentically

Respond to comments and messages the same way you would talk to someone in person. Be real, be grateful, and be helpful.

When someone takes the time to comment on your post or message you, they're giving you an opportunity to build a relationship. Don't waste it with generic responses.

Share Your Journey, Not Just Your Products

People follow people, not just products. Share:

- Your wins and challenges
- Behind-the-scenes moments
- Lessons you're learning

- Your bigger vision

My grandmother told me before she passed, "Boy, you gonna be on that stage." When I share that story and how it motivates me, people connect with my mission beyond just buying a hat.

Create Value Beyond Your Products

Give people reasons to follow you even if they're not ready to buy yet:

- Share motivational content
- Offer tips for young entrepreneurs
- Post about your faith if that's part of your brand
- Celebrate others who are grinding like you

When you consistently provide value, people will support you when they're ready to make a purchase.

Collaborate With Others

Find other entrepreneurs or content creators who share your values and audience, but aren't direct competitors. Collaborations can expose you to new followers and create win-win opportunities.

In the interview, I mentioned how being around Neo, Meet, Wolf, and Ash has given me exposure. These kinds of connections can be game-changers for your digital presence.

FROM FOLLOWERS TO CUSTOMERS

Having followers is good. Having customers is better. Here's how to convert one into the other:

The Digital Sales Funnel

Think of your online presence as a funnel:

1. **Awareness:** People discover you through content, hashtags, or shares
2. **Interest:** They follow you and engage with your content
3. **Consideration:** They visit your store or website
4. **Purchase:** They buy your product
5. **Loyalty:** They become repeat customers and advocates

Your content should move people through this funnel by addressing their needs at each stage.

Creating Urgency

Online, it's easy for people to think, "I'll buy it later" and then forget. Create urgency with:

- Limited-time offers
- Limited edition products
- Special bundles
- Early-bird discounts

For example, I might post: "Just got a new shipment of pink 'Without God I'm Nothing' hats! Only 10 available and they sold out last time. DM to reserve yours now."

Make Buying Easy

Reduce friction in the buying process:

- Include direct links to purchase in your bio and stories
- Accept multiple forms of payment
- Make shipping information clear
- Respond quickly to purchase inquiries

The fewer steps between interest and purchase, the more sales you'll make.

GETTING REPEAT CUSTOMERS THROUGH FOLLOW-UP

In person, I might make one sale to a customer. Online, I can turn one sale into many through effective follow-up.

Email Marketing

Collect email addresses (with permission) from your customers and send them:

- New product announcements
- Special offers for existing customers
- Updates on your journey
- Thank you messages

A simple "Thank you for supporting my dream" email can go a long way toward building loyalty.

Personalized Messages

When someone buys from you online, send them a direct message thanking them personally. This creates the same connection you would make in person and makes them more likely to buy again.

Share Customer Stories

When customers share photos with your products or positive feedback, ask permission to share it on your page. This creates a sense of community and provides social proof for new potential customers.

BALANCING ONLINE AND OFFLINE HUSTLE

The most successful entrepreneurs don't choose between digital and physical—they leverage both.

Cross-Promotion

When you're selling in person:

- Ask customers to follow you online
- Have QR codes that link to your social media
- Take photos with customers (with permission) to share online

When you're promoting online:

- Share where you'll be selling in person
- Post highlights from in-person events
- Create excitement for upcoming appearances

Consistent Branding

Your online presence should feel like an extension of your in-person experience:

- Use the same language and energy
- Maintain consistent pricing
- Keep your core message the same

I'm the same person online as I am when I approach you in a parking lot—passionate about my mission and grateful for your support.

Let Each Platform Do What It Does Best

Different platforms serve different purposes:

- In-person selling creates deep connections and immediate cash flow
- Instagram builds your brand and community
- Your online store provides passive income opportunities
- Email nurtures long-term customer relationships

Don't try to make one platform do everything. Use each for what it does best.

ACTION STEPS:

1. **Digital Presence Audit:** If you already have social media accounts, review them to ensure they represent your brand effectively. If not, create business accounts on the platforms where your potential customers spend time.

2. **Content Calendar:** Plan one week of content with at least one post per day. Include a mix of product highlights, behind-the-scenes moments, and your personal journey.

3. **Online Store Setup:** Choose one platform (Instagram Shop, Shopify, or even just a Square payment link) and set up the basics for online sales.

4. **Community Building:** Identify 10-20 accounts in your niche and engage meaningfully with their content. This builds visibility and connections in your digital community.

5. **Cross-Promotion Plan:** Create three specific ways you'll connect your in-person hustle with your online presence.

The digital world offers unlimited potential to scale your hustle beyond what's physically possible. But remember—the principles that make you successful on the sidewalk are the same ones that make you successful online: confidence, authenticity, and providing value beyond just your product.

The streets may have taught us how to hustle, but the screens can help us build an empire.

CHAPTER 5

THE LEGAL TRAP TEAM

SCALING BEYOND YOURSELF

No matter how good you get at selling, there's always a limit to what you can do alone. Even hustling 12 hours a day, you can only be in one place at a time. You can only speak to so many people. You can only make so many sales.

That's why the next level of hustling isn't just getting better—it's getting bigger.

In the streets, they call it "building a trap team." Someone with product gives it to others on consignment (meaning they don't pay upfront), those people sell it, and then they split the profits. This system has built some of the biggest illegal operations in urban communities.

But here's the thing: the system itself isn't illegal. It's the product that makes it illegal. The strategy—the concept of consignment, team building, and scaling through others—is just smart business.

That's what we're going to do: take the trap team concept and make it 100% legal. We'll build what I call a "Legal Trap Team"—a group of motivated sellers who help you scale your hustle while everyone profits.

HOW CONSIGNMENT WORKS (AND HOW TO FLIP THE MODEL LEGALLY)

Consignment is simple: you give your product to someone else to sell, and they only pay you after they make the sale. Here's how it typically works:

1. You provide the product upfront
2. They sell it at a markup
3. They keep some of the profit
4. They give you the rest

In illegal operations, this creates a dangerous power dynamic where the supplier has leverage over the seller. But we're going to flip that dynamic to create opportunity, not dependency.

Here's my legal consignment model:

For the hats I sell:

- My cost: $5 per hat
- I sell them directly: $15 per hat ($10 profit)
- I sell to team members: $5-$7 per hat (no/small profit)
- They sell to customers: $15-$20 per hat ($8-$15 profit for them)

Instead of trying to make money from my team, I make money from volume. By having multiple people selling, I can order more hats at once, potentially lowering my cost per hat. Plus, I'm building a brand and reputation that goes beyond just my personal sales.

The key difference in my legal model is that I'm genuinely interested in my team members' success. I want them to make more than me on each individual sale because their success is my success in the long run.

RECRUITING THE RIGHT TEAM MEMBERS

Not everyone is cut out to be on your team. I've had plenty of friends say, "Man, I don't know how to sell a product like you," even after I've tried to teach them. Finding the right people is crucial.

Here's what I look for:

Determination: They need to have hunger—a reason why they're hustling. Without that internal drive, they'll quit at the first rejection.

Positivity: Negative energy drives customers away. I need people who can stay upbeat even when facing rejection.

Willingness to Learn: As I told Ash in our interview, "I know I don't know everything. I'm just a sponge. I just want game." Look for people with this mindset—those who don't think they already know everything.

Reliability: If someone can't show up on time or follow through on commitments, they'll hurt your brand more than help it.

Complementary Skills: Some people might not be great at approaching strangers but excel at social media. Others might be natural salespeople but terrible at organization. Look for people whose strengths complement your weaknesses.

Where do you find these people? Start with:

1. **Friends and Family:** People you already know and trust
2. **School or Work Connections:** Classmates or colleagues who show hustle
3. **Other Hustlers:** People already selling (legal products) in your area
4. **Social Media:** Followers who consistently engage with your content

When approaching potential team members, be honest about what you're offering. Don't promise overnight riches. Instead, offer a legitimate opportunity to learn sales skills while making money.

TRAINING YOUR TEAM

You can't just hand someone your product and expect them to succeed. Proper training is essential for both their success and your reputation.

Here's how I train new team members:

1. Shadow First

Have them spend a day watching you sell. Let them see how you approach people, handle objections, and close sales. This gives them a real-world model to follow.

I'll have them count how many people I approach and how many sales I make. This helps them understand that rejection is normal and that sales is a numbers game.

2. Script Development

Help them develop their own sales script based on yours, but tailored to their personality and style. It should include:

- A respectful greeting
- Who they are and what they're selling
- The purpose behind the product
- A clear ask for the sale

The script shouldn't sound robotic—it should be a framework they can personalize.

3. Role Play

Practice with them before they approach real customers. Take turns playing the customer and throw different objections at them:

- "I don't have cash"
- "I'm in a rush"
- "I already have too many hats"
- "Why should I buy this?"

The more they practice responding to objections, the more confident they'll be in real situations.

4. Supervised Sales

Go with them for their first few sales attempts. Let them lead the interaction, but be there to jump in if needed. After each attempt, give specific feedback:

- What they did well
- What they could improve
- How to handle specific objections better

This real-time coaching is invaluable for rapid improvement.

5. Gradual Independence

As they gain confidence and competence, give them more independence. Maybe they start in the same location as you but approach people on their own. Eventually, they can work different locations or events.

Remember, their performance reflects on your brand. It's better to spend extra time training them properly than to have them out there representing you poorly.

HOW TO PAY YOUR TEAM AND TRACK PROGRESS

Clear payment structures and tracking systems are essential for any team. Without them, misunderstandings and disputes are inevitable.

Payment Options

There are several ways to structure payments:

Straight Commission: Team members keep a percentage of each sale. For example, if they sell a hat for $15 and their commission is 60%, they keep $9 and give you $6.

Tiered Commission: Commission rates increase as they sell more units. For example:

- 1-5 hats: 50% commission
- 6-10 hats: 60% commission
- 11+ hats: 70% commission

This incentivizes higher volume.

Wholesale Model: They buy from you at a fixed price (like $7 per hat) and keep all the profit when they sell at a higher price (like $15-$20).

I prefer the wholesale model because it's simpler to track and creates true entrepreneurship. My team members aren't just working for me—they're building their own micro-businesses.

Tracking Systems

You need a simple system to track inventory, sales, and performance:

Inventory Tracking: Know exactly how many products each team member has. A simple spreadsheet or even a notebook can work.

Sales Reporting: Have team members report their sales daily or weekly. This helps you identify who needs more training or support.

Performance Metrics: Track not just total sales, but also:

- Conversion rate (sales divided by approaches)
- Average sale amount (if you sell multiple products)
- Peak selling times and locations

You can use basic tools like Google Sheets or specialized apps like Square to keep track of these metrics.

Example Tracking Setup

Here's a simple system I use:

1. Create a spreadsheet with team member names in rows
2. Add columns for:
   - Inventory out
   - Inventory returned
   - Units sold
   - Total sales amount
   - Commission earned
   - Notes/feedback

Update this after each selling session or at the end of each day.

Remember, what gets measured gets improved. Team members who see their performance tracked will naturally work to improve their numbers.

KEEPING YOUR TEAM MOTIVATED

Getting people to join your team is one thing. Keeping them motivated and productive is another challenge entirely. Here's how I keep my team fired up:

Financial Incentives

Money is an obvious motivator, but how you structure financial incentives matters:

Contests and Bonuses: Create friendly competition with prizes for the top seller of the week or month.

Performance Milestones: Offer bonuses when team members hit certain sales targets.

Increased Rates for Consistency: Reward team members who show up consistently by giving them better rates or first access to new products.

Recognition and Respect

People want to feel valued beyond just the money they make:

Public Recognition: Highlight top performers on your social media or in team meetings.

Responsibility Growth: Give successful team members more responsibility, like training new recruits or managing certain locations.

Ask for Input: Make team members feel invested by asking for their ideas on new products, selling locations, or strategies.

Personal Development

The best team members want to grow beyond just making money:

Skills Training: Offer training not just in sales, but in other business skills like social media marketing or financial management.

Mentorship: Connect promising team members with other successful entrepreneurs or resources.

Vision Sharing: Help them see how being on your team can help them achieve their own long-term goals.

Team Culture

Create a positive environment that people want to be part of:

Team Activities: Organize occasional non-work activities to build relationships.

Shared Values: Emphasize positive values like integrity, growth, and supporting each other.

Celebration of Wins: Take time to celebrate team and individual achievements.

I always make sure my team knows that I'm not just interested in what they can do for me, but in helping them grow. When someone sees you genuinely care about their success, they'll work harder and stay loyal longer.

LEADERSHIP 101: RESPECT, REWARDS, AND REAL COMMUNICATION

Building a team isn't just about systems and strategies—it's about leadership. Here are the leadership principles I live by:

Respect Goes Both Ways

Respect is the foundation of any successful team:

Respect Their Time: Be punctual for meetings and responsive to messages.

Respect Their Intelligence: Explain the "why" behind your requests and rules.

Respect Their Circumstances: Understand that everyone has personal challenges and be reasonable with expectations.

Demand Respect in Return: While being understanding, also maintain clear standards for how team members should treat you and each other.

Communication That Actually Works

Miscommunication kills teams faster than almost anything else:

Be Clear and Direct: Don't hint at what you want—say it clearly.

Listen Actively: When team members speak, really listen to understand, not just to respond.

Regular Check-ins: Have consistent one-on-one conversations with each team member to address concerns and give feedback.

Accessible Leadership: Make yourself available to answer questions and provide guidance.

Lead by Example

Nothing undermines leadership faster than hypocrisy:

Work Ethic: Never ask your team to work harder than you do.

Integrity: If you say you'll do something, do it without exception.

Continuous Learning: Show that you're always improving your own skills.

Positive Attitude: Maintain the same positive energy you expect from your team.

Remember, your team is watching you closely. They'll follow what you do much more than what you say.

MANAGING CHALLENGES AND CONFLICTS

No team operates without challenges. How you handle them determines whether they strengthen or weaken your organization:

Common Team Challenges

Inconsistent Performance: Some team members will start strong but taper off. Address performance issues promptly through one-on-one conversations focusing on specific behaviors and solutions.

Inter-Team Conflicts: Personalities may clash, or competition can turn unhealthy. Establish clear conflict resolution procedures and address issues before they escalate.

Theft or Dishonesty: Unfortunately, some people may try to take advantage by misreporting sales or stealing inventory. Have systems in place to track inventory and verify sales.

Burnout: Hustling is hard work, and people can burn out. Watch for signs of fatigue and encourage breaks when needed.

When to Let Someone Go

Not everyone will work out on your team. It's important to know when to part ways:

Repeated Rule Violations: If someone consistently breaks rules despite warnings, they're damaging your brand.

Toxic Attitude: Someone who brings negative energy can demoralize the entire team.

Dishonesty: Trust is essential; once broken, it's very difficult to rebuild.

Persistent Underperformance: If someone continues to struggle despite additional training and support, the position may not be right for them.

When letting someone go, do it respectfully and privately. Explain your reasons clearly and wish them well. How you treat people on their way out says as much about your leadership as how you treat them when they're performing well.

LEGAL CONSIDERATIONS FOR YOUR TEAM

Building a legal trap team means paying attention to the legal aspects of team management:

Independent Contractors vs. Employees

In most cases, your team members will be independent contractors, not employees. This means:

- They control their own schedule and how they do the work
- They use their own methods to make sales
- They don't receive benefits like health insurance
- They're responsible for their own taxes

Make this relationship clear from the beginning to avoid legal complications.

Written Agreements

Even with friends and family, have basic written agreements that cover:

- Commission structures or wholesale pricing
- Expectations for representing your brand
- Inventory responsibility
- Termination conditions

These don't have to be complex legal documents, but having things in writing prevents misunderstandings.

Tax Considerations

As your team grows, be aware of tax implications:

- Keep records of all payments to team members
- For payments over $600 in a year, you may need to issue 1099 forms
- Consider consulting with a tax professional as your operation grows

This might seem like unnecessary formality when you're just starting, but proper legal and tax compliance will save you headaches as you scale.

ACTION STEPS:

1. **Team Structure Planning:** Decide which payment model (commission, tiered, or wholesale) works best for your hustle and create a simple one-page document outlining how it works.
2. **Recruit Your First Team Member:** Identify one person who meets your criteria and invite them to join you for a day of selling to see if it's a good fit.
3. **Create a Basic Training Plan:** Outline the specific steps you'll use to train new team members, from shadowing to independent sales.
4. **Develop a Tracking System:** Set up a simple spreadsheet or notebook to track inventory and sales for each team member.
5. **Leadership Self-Assessment:** Identify your strengths and weaknesses as a leader and one specific leadership skill you want to improve.

Building a legal trap team isn't just about making more money—it's about creating opportunities for others while scaling your vision. When done right, your team becomes a network of people all rising together, breaking those generational curses we talked about and creating new possibilities for everyone involved.

Remember: In the streets, trap teams are built on fear and control. Our legal trap teams are built on opportunity and growth. That's the difference between a hustle that leads to trouble and a hustle that leads to transformation.

CHAPTER 6

SYSTEMS = FREEDOM

WHY SYSTEMS MATTER

When I first started selling hats, I was doing everything by feel. I didn't track my inventory systematically. I didn't have a formal process for approaching customers. I didn't have organized methods for handling my money.

I was hustling, but I was hustling hard, not smart.

What changed everything for me was understanding one simple truth: **Systems equal freedom**.

Most people think systems are boring. They think systems mean rules, restrictions, and routine. But the reality is exactly the opposite. Good systems don't limit you—they liberate you.

When you have systems in place:

- You don't have to stress about remembering everything
- You make fewer costly mistakes

- You can focus your creativity where it matters
- You can scale without everything falling apart
- You can delegate with confidence

Think about it this way: Without systems, you're a one-person show that only runs when you're on stage. With systems, you're building something that can run even when you're not there.

That's real freedom. That's real power.

SIMPLE SYSTEMS FOR INVENTORY MANAGEMENT

Inventory might seem simple—you buy products, you sell products. But without proper systems, inventory problems can sink your hustle fast.

Here's what can go wrong without an inventory system:

- You run out of popular items and miss sales
- You order too much of items that don't sell well
- You lose track of what you've given to team members
- You don't know if items are going missing or being stolen
- You tie up too much money in unsold inventory

My inventory system started simple and has grown more sophisticated over time. Here's how you can build yours:

The Basic Inventory Tracker

In its simplest form, your inventory system can be a notebook with four columns:

1. **Date**
2. **Product In** (what you bought or received)
3. **Product Out** (what you sold or distributed to team)
4. **Current Count** (what you have left)

Update this daily, and you'll always know where you stand.

Digital Inventory Tracking

As you grow, consider upgrading to a digital system:

- Google Sheets is free and can be accessed from any device
- Square has built-in inventory tracking that connects to sales
- Dedicated inventory apps provide more features as you scale

For my hat business, I use Google Sheets with columns for:

- Product name and color
- Quantity on hand
- Quantity with each team member
- Reorder point (when I need to buy more)
- Supplier information
- Cost per unit
- Selling price
- Profit margin

I update this at the end of each day, which takes less than five minutes but saves hours of headaches.

Inventory Rules to Live By

No matter what system you use, follow these principles:

- **First In, First Out (FIFO):** Sell older inventory before newer inventory, especially for products that can show wear
- **Set Reorder Points:** Decide in advance at what quantity you'll reorder more product
- **Regular Counts:** Physically count your inventory weekly to catch any discrepancies
- **Quality Checks:** Regularly inspect products for damage or defects
- **Seasonal Planning:** Anticipate busy seasons and stock up accordingly

With a solid inventory system, you'll never be caught off guard by shortages or overstock. You'll always know exactly what you have and what you need.

MONEY MANAGEMENT SYSTEMS THAT KEEP YOU PROFITABLE

Making money is one thing. Managing money is another skill entirely. Without good money management systems, you can be hustling hard but still find yourself broke.

Here's my approach to money management:

The Three Accounts System

At minimum, you need three separate accounts:

1. **Business Operations:** For buying inventory, paying expenses, and running your hustle
2. **Profit Account:** For your personal pay and rewards
3. **Tax Account:** For setting aside money to pay taxes

When money comes in, I immediately divide it:

- 60% goes to Business Operations
- 30% goes to Profit
- 10% goes to Taxes

This system ensures I always have money to restock inventory, I get paid for my work, and I don't get surprised by tax bills.

Daily Cash Handling

When you're selling on the streets, you're dealing with cash. Cash is great, but it's easy to lose track of. My system is:

1. **Separate Storage:** Keep sales money completely separate from personal money
2. **End-of-Day Counts:** Count all cash at the end of each day
3. **Regular Deposits:** Don't keep large amounts of cash on hand—deposit it in your bank accounts
4. **Sales Log:** Record each sale as it happens (Square makes this easy)
5. **Receipt Discipline:** Keep receipts for all business expenses

This system prevents the all-too-common problem of money "disappearing" from your hustle.

Pricing Strategy

Your pricing isn't just a number—it's a system. For my hats:

- My cost: $5
- My selling price: $15
- Team member wholesale price: $7

This system ensures I have a 66% profit margin when I sell directly and a 28% margin on wholesale to my team. These margins give me room to cover all expenses while still making profit.

Whatever you sell, your pricing system should include:

- Your cost (including shipping, packaging, etc.)
- Your target profit margin
- Different price points for different channels (direct, team, online, etc.)
- Any discount structures for volume purchases

With this system, you'll know instantly if a deal is profitable or not.

Expense Tracking

Every dollar you spend on your business needs to be tracked. My system includes:

- Taking photos of all receipts with my phone

- Categorizing expenses (inventory, supplies, transportation, etc.)
- Weekly review of all expenses
- Monthly calculation of total expenses vs. revenue

This system helps me identify where money is being wasted and where I might need to invest more.

LOGISTICS SYSTEMS THAT SAVE TIME AND HEADACHES

Logistics might sound complicated, but it's simply about moving your products efficiently from suppliers to customers. Good logistics systems eliminate wasted time and effort.

Supplier Management

Develop a system for working with suppliers:

- Keep contact information for multiple suppliers
- Know each supplier's lead times (how long orders take)
- Track quality and reliability
- Develop relationships for better terms

For my hat business, I have three different suppliers. If one has delays or quality issues, I can quickly pivot to another.

Delivery and Shipping

As you expand beyond in-person sales, you'll need systems for getting products to customers:

- Standard packaging materials
- Consistent shipping methods
- Tracking information for all shipments
- Clear delivery timeframes

Even for local deliveries, have a system—specific days for deliveries, organized routes, and confirmation procedures.

Event Planning

For selling at events, create a checklist system:

- Inventory needed
- Display equipment
- Payment processing tools
- Marketing materials
- Transportation arrangements
- Setup and breakdown procedures

I have this entire checklist in my phone. Before any event, I run through it to make sure I'm fully prepared.

TOOLS AND APPS I USE EVERY DAY

You don't need fancy technology to create good systems, but the right tools can make your systems more efficient. Here are the tools that help run my hustle:

Google Sheets

I use Google Sheets for:

- Tracking inventory
- Recording sales data
- Managing team member performance
- Planning marketing content

The best part is it's free and accessible from any device.

Square

Square helps me:

- Accept credit card payments through my phone
- Track cash sales
- Send digital receipts
- Analyze sales patterns

The basic service has no monthly fee—they only charge a small percentage of each transaction.

Cash App and Venmo

These payment apps let me:

- Accept payments from customers who don't have cash
- Pay suppliers quickly
- Transfer money between my accounts

- Pay team members immediately

Having multiple payment options means never missing a sale because of payment method.

Calendar Apps

I use Google Calendar to:

- Schedule selling locations and times
- Plan inventory ordering
- Set reminders for following up with potential partners
- Block time for systems maintenance and review

This keeps me organized and ensures nothing falls through the cracks.

Note-Taking Apps

I use the notes app on my phone to:

- Record new sales approaches to try
- Track customer feedback
- Jot down ideas for new products
- Keep lists of potential selling locations

Having these notes organized and searchable means good ideas don't get lost.

WORKING ON YOUR HUSTLE, NOT JUST IN IT

There's a critical difference between working IN your hustle and working ON your hustle:

- Working IN your hustle means doing the day-to-day tasks: selling products, handling customers, managing inventory
- Working ON your hustle means improving your systems, planning strategy, and building for the future

Most hustlers never make this transition. They stay trapped working IN their business, which means:

- They're always busy
- Growth is limited by their personal time and energy
- The business depends entirely on them
- They can't take time off without losing money

To break this cycle, schedule specific time to work ON your business:

- Weekly: 1-2 hours to review and adjust immediate systems
- Monthly: Half a day to analyze broader patterns and plan improvements
- Quarterly: A full day to think strategically about bigger opportunities

During these sessions, focus on questions like:

- Which systems are working well, and which need improvement?
- What tasks am I doing that could be systematized or delegated?

- What opportunities am I missing because I'm too busy with day-to-day operations?
- How can I increase profitability without working more hours?

This time investment pays massive dividends. Every hour spent improving your systems can save you dozens or hundreds of hours of work later.

THE FREEDOM THAT COMES FROM SYSTEMS

Good systems create freedom in multiple ways:

Mental Freedom

When your business runs on systems instead of constant decisions, you free up mental space. You're not constantly stressed about forgetting something or making mistakes. This mental clarity is invaluable for creativity and strategic thinking.

Time Freedom

Systems automate routine tasks and make everything more efficient. This means you can handle more volume without working more hours, or maintain your current volume while working fewer hours.

For me, good systems turned a 12-hour day into an 8-hour day while actually increasing my profits.

Financial Freedom

Systematic approaches to inventory, pricing, and money management lead directly to higher profits. You waste less, sell more efficiently, and make better financial decisions.

Growth Freedom

With solid systems, you can grow without everything falling apart. You can add team members, new products, or new locations because you have frameworks that scale.

Future Freedom

Perhaps most importantly, systems turn your hustle from a job into an asset. A hustle that depends entirely on you has limited value to anyone else. A hustle with strong systems that can run without you is something that could potentially be sold or handed off in the future.

BALANCING SYSTEMS AND FLEXIBILITY

Some hustlers resist systems because they fear losing creativity or the ability to adapt. But the right systems actually enhance these qualities.

Think of systems as the foundation and structure of your hustle—they provide stability but don't dictate every detail. Within your systems, there's plenty of room for:

- Creative approaches to individual sales

- Testing new products or strategies
- Responding to unexpected opportunities
- Expressing your unique personality and style

In fact, good systems free you to be more creative where it counts, because you're not wasting creative energy on routine tasks.

The key is building systems that support your hustle rather than constrain it. Review your systems regularly and ask: "Is this helping me achieve my goals more efficiently, or is it getting in the way?" If it's the latter, the system needs adjustment.

ACTION STEPS:

1. **System Audit:** List all the activities in your hustle and identify which ones have formal systems and which are done by "feel" or memory. Choose one area without a system to formalize this week.
2. **Inventory System Setup:** Create a basic inventory tracking system using either a notebook or Google Sheets. Do a complete count of your current inventory and record it.
3. **Money Management Structure:** Open separate accounts for business operations, profit, and taxes if you haven't already. Determine your percentage allocations for each.
4. **Daily Close Procedure:** Create a checklist for end-of-day activities: counting inventory, recording sales, handling cash, and preparing for the next day.
5. **ON Your Business Time:** Schedule a specific two-hour block this week dedicated solely to working ON your business systems, not IN your day-to-day operations.

Remember: Systems might not seem as exciting as making sales or launching new products, but they're the difference between a temporary hustle and a sustainable business. The time you invest in creating and refining your systems will pay off many times over.

The streets may have taught us how to hustle, but systems teach us how to build something that lasts.

CHAPTER 7

MAKE MONEY WORK FOR YOU

THE HUSTLE IS JUST THE BEGINNING

Let me tell you something I learned early that many people never figure out: The hustle isn't the endpoint—it's just the beginning.

When I started selling hats and making $800 a day, I could have easily fallen into the trap that catches so many hustlers. I could have spent that money on designer clothes, the latest phones, or trying to look rich. But I realized something important: Looking rich and becoming wealthy are two completely different paths.

The real goal isn't just to make money through your hustle—it's to make your money work for you. It's about turning your active income (money you work for) into passive income (money that works for you).

This is what separates those who build temporary success from those who create lasting wealth. This is how you break generational curses. This is how you create true financial freedom.

CEDRIC'S BLUEPRINT: FROM HUSTLE TO WEALTH

Making the transition from hustler to investor isn't complicated, but it does require discipline and vision. Here's my blueprint for turning hustle money into wealth:

Step 1: Master Your Hustle

Before you can invest, you need consistent income. This means:

- Perfecting your sales techniques
- Building reliable systems
- Developing multiple income streams through your hustle
- Creating predictable cash flow

If you're still struggling to make consistent money from your hustle, focus there first. The chapters before this one give you the foundation you need.

Step 2: Control Your Spending

You can't invest what you don't keep. While others are flexing with expensive purchases, I'm focused on my saving rate. This means:

- Living below your means, not at or above them
- Distinguishing between assets (things that make you money) and liabilities (things that cost you money)
- Being strategic about every dollar you spend
- Avoiding consumer debt completely

Remember: Every dollar you don't spend is a dollar you can invest.

Step 3: Build Your Investment Fund

Before making any investments, build a dedicated investment fund. This means:

- Setting aside a specific percentage of all income for investments
- Keeping this money separate from personal and business funds
- Being patient as it grows—don't rush into investments
- Continuing to add to it consistently, regardless of the amount

Even $50 a week adds up to $2,600 in a year—enough to make your first small passive income investment.

Step 4: Research Before You Invest

Never invest in something you don't understand. This means:

- Learning everything you can about potential investments
- Starting with simpler, lower-risk options
- Finding mentors who have succeeded with similar investments
- Testing with small amounts before making larger commitments

Knowledge is your best protection against investment failures.

Step 5: Diversify Your Investments

Don't put all your money in one type of investment. This means:

- Spreading your money across different investment types
- Balancing higher-risk with lower-risk options
- Having both short-term and long-term investment horizons
- Creating multiple streams of passive income

This approach protects you if one investment doesn't perform as expected.

Step 6: Reinvest Your Returns

The real power of investing comes from compounding. This means:

- Reinvesting the returns from your investments
- Letting your money make money, which then makes more money
- Being patient with the process—wealth building accelerates over time
- Focusing on the long-term growth, not just immediate returns

This is how small investments eventually turn into significant wealth.

Step 7: Scale with Experience

As your knowledge and confidence grow, scale your investments. This means:

- Increasing the amount you invest as your income grows
- Taking on more complex investments as you gain experience
- Leveraging your growing network for better opportunities
- Staying educated about new investment options

Your investment strategy should evolve as you evolve.

WHAT IS PASSIVE INCOME (AND WHAT IT'S NOT)

There's a lot of confusion about what passive income really is. Let me clear that up.

Passive income is money earned with minimal ongoing effort after an initial investment of time, money, or both. The key word is "minimal"—not "zero."

What Passive Income IS:

- Money that continues to flow when you're not actively working
- Income that scales without requiring proportionately more of your time
- Revenue that comes from assets you own or control
- Earnings that grow through systems and other people's efforts

What Passive Income IS NOT:

- Completely effort-free money (every passive income stream requires some maintenance)
- Get-rich-quick schemes or overnight success
- A replacement for hard work (passive income usually starts with active effort)
- A guarantee (all investments carry some level of risk)

Understanding this distinction is crucial. Too many people chase the fantasy of money for nothing, while successful wealth builders focus on creating assets that generate ongoing returns with decreasing personal effort over time.

THE "3-STACK RULE": SPEND, SAVE, INVEST

One of the simplest but most powerful systems I use is what I call the "3-Stack Rule" for managing money. Here's how it works:

Whenever money comes in, I immediately divide it into three stacks:

Stack 1: SPEND (50%) - This covers:

- Living expenses
- Business costs
- Some enjoyment (because life should be lived)

Stack 2: SAVE (20%) - This provides:

- Emergency fund (3-6 months of expenses)
- Major purchase planning
- Security and peace of mind

Stack 3: INVEST (30%) - This builds:

- Passive income assets
- Long-term wealth
- Financial freedom

These percentages can be adjusted based on your situation, but the principle remains the same: every dollar has a purpose before it hits your hand.

This system prevents the common problem of investing whatever's "left over" at the end of the month—which for most people is nothing. By prioritizing investing and saving from the start, you ensure they actually happen.

I implement this system immediately when I get paid. If I make $800 in a day selling hats:

- $400 goes to spending (business and personal)
- $160 goes to savings
- $240 goes to investments

Over time, these consistent allocations add up to significant results.

WEALTH ISN'T FAST—IT'S FOREVER

Let me be completely straight with you: Building real wealth takes time. Anyone promising you fast riches is either lying or suggesting something illegal or extremely risky.

The wealth-building journey typically follows this timeline:

Years 1-3: This is the foundation phase where you're establishing your hustle, creating systems, and starting to save and make small investments. Progress often feels slow during this period.

Years 3-7: This is the growth phase where your knowledge, network, and initial investments start to gain momentum. You begin to see more substantial results from your efforts.

Years 7-15: This is the acceleration phase where compound returns really kick in. Your passive income starts to approach and potentially exceed your active income.

Years 15+: This is the freedom phase where your investments generate enough income to cover your lifestyle without requiring you to work.

Of course, these timelines can vary based on factors like:

- How much you can invest
- The types of investments you make
- How disciplined you are with your money
- How much you learn and improve your strategies
- The opportunities available in your network

The point is not to get discouraged by the timeline, but to understand that real wealth is built through consistent action over time. Every day you delay starting is a day of compound returns you'll never get back.

Remember what I said earlier: Nobody in my family has ever been a millionaire or financially free. I'm breaking that generational curse not by looking for shortcuts, but by understanding that wealth isn't fast—it's forever.

STARTING SMALL: INVESTMENT MINDSET FOR BEGINNERS

You don't need a lot of money to start investing, but you do need the right mindset. Here's how to think like an investor even when you're just getting started:

See Money as a Tool, Not a Toy

Money is a tool for building freedom, not a toy for temporary pleasure. Every dollar you spend on something that loses value is a dollar that can't work for you.

When I first started making good money, I was tempted to buy expensive clothes or the latest tech. Instead, I focused on asking: "Will this purchase help me make more money or just cost me money?"

Think in Terms of Net Worth, Not Income

Many hustlers focus entirely on how much they make, but what matters more is how much you keep and grow. Your net worth (what you own minus what you owe) is a better measure of financial progress than income.

I track my net worth monthly to see if I'm moving in the right direction. Even small increases add up over time.

Prioritize Financial Education

The best investment you can make when starting out is in your financial knowledge. This doesn't mean expensive courses or seminars—it means books, free online resources, and conversations with people who are successfully doing what you want to do.

I listen to financial podcasts while I'm driving to selling locations and read investment books when I'm not hustling. This education helps me avoid costly mistakes and identify better opportunities.

Embrace Delayed Gratification

The ability to say "not yet" to things you want now is crucial for building wealth. This doesn't mean never enjoying your money—it means being strategic about when and how you reward yourself.

I set specific financial milestones and small rewards for reaching them, rather than spending impulsively. This keeps me motivated while still prioritizing growth.

Be Patient with the Process

Investment returns often follow a J-curve—they might seem flat or even negative at first before curving upward into significant growth. Having realistic expectations prevents you from giving up too soon.

Understanding this pattern helps me stay committed even when results aren't immediately visible.

INVESTMENT OPTIONS FOR YOUNG HUSTLERS

As a young entrepreneur with limited capital, you need investment options that:

- Have relatively low barriers to entry
- Provide cash flow rather than just long-term appreciation
- Allow you to leverage your hustle skills
- Diversify your income streams

Here are several options worth considering, starting from the simplest:

High-Yield Savings Accounts and CDs

While not exciting, these provide safe places for your first savings:

- Minimal risk (FDIC insured)
- Low minimum deposits
- Easy access to funds if needed
- Better returns than regular savings accounts

Consider these for your emergency fund and short-term savings.

Retirement Accounts

Even at a young age, start thinking about retirement accounts:

- Roth IRA: Especially good for young people in lower tax brackets
- SEP IRA: For self-employed individuals
- Solo 401(k): Another good option for self-employed entrepreneurs

These accounts provide tax advantages that enhance your returns over time.

Fractional Real Estate Investing

Real estate investments are no longer limited to those who can afford entire properties:

- Real estate crowdfunding platforms let you invest with as little as $10
- REITs (Real Estate Investment Trusts) allow you to buy shares in income-producing real estate
- Partnership opportunities may exist within your network

These options give you exposure to real estate returns without requiring large upfront investments.

Dividend-Paying Stocks

Companies that share profits with shareholders can provide regular income:

- Look for established companies with history of dividend payments
- Reinvest dividends to buy more shares automatically
- Consider dividend-focused ETFs for diversification

These investments can grow in value while also providing cash flow.

Small Business Investments

Sometimes the best investments are in businesses you understand:

- Expanding your own business with new products or locations
- Investing in other local entrepreneurs you know and trust
- Providing inventory or equipment to other hustlers in exchange for revenue share

These investments leverage your existing knowledge and network.

Creating Digital Products

Once you've built knowledge and credibility, create products that sell while you sleep:

- E-books sharing your expertise
- Online courses teaching your skills
- Templates or tools others in your industry would pay for

These have high margins and can generate income for years with minimal ongoing effort.

PROTECTING YOUR GROWING WEALTH

As your wealth increases, protecting it becomes increasingly important. Here are strategies to safeguard what you're building:

Legal Structures

As your investments grow, consider creating legal structures that protect your assets:

- LLC (Limited Liability Company) for business activities
- Separate entities for different investment types
- Proper insurance coverage for all assets

Consult with a professional to determine the right structures for your situation.

Tax Strategy

Taxes can significantly impact your returns. Develop a basic understanding of:

- Tax-advantaged investment accounts
- Legitimate business deductions
- Record-keeping requirements
- Estimated tax payments for self-employed individuals

Consider working with a tax professional as your investments become more complex.

Diversification

Never put all your money in one type of investment. Spread your investments across:

- Different asset classes (stocks, real estate, business)
- Multiple specific investments within each class
- Varying levels of risk and return
- Different time horizons

This approach ensures that a failure in one area won't devastate your entire portfolio.

Continuous Education

The investment landscape constantly changes. Stay educated about:

- New investment opportunities
- Changes in tax laws and regulations
- Economic trends that might affect your investments
- Additional skills that enhance your earning potential

The more you know, the better you can protect and grow your wealth.

ACTION STEPS:

1. **3-Stack Implementation:** Start implementing the 3-Stack Rule immediately. Set up separate accounts for spending, saving, and investing if you haven't already, and automatically direct your income into these accounts based on your chosen percentages.

2. **Investment Fund Starter:** Open a high-yield savings account specifically for your investment fund. Commit to depositing a specific amount weekly, no matter how small.

3. **Financial Education Plan:** Select one book about investing to read this month. (Recommendations: "Rich Dad Poor Dad" by Robert Kiyosaki, "The Simple Path to Wealth" by JL Collins, or "I Will Teach You to Be Rich" by Ramit Sethi)

4. **Net Worth Tracker:** Create a simple spreadsheet listing all your assets (what you own) and liabilities (what you owe). Calculate your current net worth and commit to updating it monthly.

5. **Investment Research:** Pick one type of passive income investment from this chapter that interests you. Spend two hours researching the basics of how it works, what it costs to start, and what returns you might expect.

Remember, converting your hustle into lasting wealth isn't about getting lucky with one big score—it's about consistent application of smart principles over time. The disciplined implementation of these steps will put you far ahead of most people, regardless of your starting point or age.

The streets may have taught us how to hustle, but strategic investing teaches us how to build a legacy.

CHAPTER 8

LOW-KEY PASSIVE INCOME PLAYS

TURNING YOUR HUSTLE PROFITS INTO ONGOING INCOME

When people think about investing, they often picture Wall Street, complicated stock charts, or real estate empires. But the truth is, there are plenty of "low-key" passive income opportunities that don't require a finance degree or millions of dollars to get started.

These are the kinds of investments I'm focusing on with my hat business profits. They're accessible. They're understandable. And most importantly, they create cash flow without requiring me to work for every dollar.

In this chapter, I'll break down several passive income plays that have low barriers to entry, meaning you can start with a few thousand dollars rather than tens or hundreds of thousands. These are investments where your hustle skills—sales, people skills, work ethic—give you an advantage over typical investors.

Remember: The goal isn't to replace your hustle immediately. It's to gradually build income streams that work alongside your hustle until eventually, they can work instead of your hustle.

VENDING MACHINES: THE 24/7 SILENT SALESMAN

Vending machines are one of my favorite passive income plays because they combine physical assets with automated sales—something that connects perfectly with my experience as a street hustler.

How Vending Machines Make Money

The business model is beautifully simple:

1. You buy a machine and products to stock it
2. You place the machine in a location with good foot traffic
3. People insert money and receive products
4. You collect the cash and restock periodically

The profit comes from the markup on products. For example, you might buy sodas for $0.50 each and sell them for $1.50, creating a $1.00 profit per sale. Multiply that by dozens of sales per day, and you have a nice income stream.

Startup Costs

Getting started with vending machines can be more affordable than you might think:

- Used machines: $500-$2,000
- New machines: $2,000-$4,000
- Initial inventory: $300-$1,000
- Tools and supplies: $100-$200

For around $3,000, you could have your first vending machine business up and running. This is achievable after a few months of consistent profits from your primary hustle.

Finding Locations

The key to vending machine success is location. Great places to consider include:

- Apartment complexes (laundry rooms are ideal)
- Small offices or warehouses
- Auto repair shops
- Hair salons and barber shops
- Gyms and recreation centers
- Community colleges

These locations typically have less competition than major retail spots, which often have exclusive contracts with big vending companies.

Your approach to securing locations should leverage your sales skills. Offer location owners a small percentage of sales (10-15%) or a flat monthly fee. Create a simple one-page proposal explaining the benefits to them: added convenience for their customers or employees, extra income with zero work, and a professional service they don't have to manage.

Maintenance and Restocking

The "passive" part of this income isn't completely hands-off. You'll need to:

- Check machines 1-2 times per week
- Restock inventory as needed
- Collect money (unless you have cashless payment systems)
- Address any mechanical issues
- Track sales and profitability

For one machine, this might take 1-2 hours per week. As you add more machines, you can create more efficient routes and systems.

Scaling Up

The beauty of vending machines is that they scale linearly:

- One machine might net $200-$400 per month
- Five machines could generate $1,000-$2,000 monthly
- Ten machines could bring in $2,000-$4,000 monthly

Each machine you add creates another income stream without requiring proportionately more time. Your first machine teaches you the business; each additional machine leverages what you've already learned.

Getting Started

To get started with vending machines:

1. Research machine types and products that sell well in your area

2. Join vending machine groups on social media to learn from others

3. Look for used machines on Facebook Marketplace, Craigslist, or from local vendors

4. Create a simple business plan outlining your startup costs and projected returns

5. Identify 10-15 potential locations and prepare your pitch

6. Start with one machine, master it, then expand

Remember, the goal is to start small, learn the business thoroughly, then scale up as your knowledge and capital allow.

ATM MACHINES: BANKING ON CONVENIENCE

ATM machines are similar to vending machines in concept, but instead of dispensing products, they dispense cash—and charge a fee for the convenience.

How ATM Machines Work and Make Money

The business model works like this:

1. You purchase an ATM and load it with cash

2. You place it in a location where people need access to cash

3. Users withdraw money and pay a service fee (typically $2.50-$5.00)

4. You keep the service fees as your profit

For example, if your fee is $3.00 and you get 20 transactions per day, that's $60 daily or approximately $1,800 monthly in revenue.

Startup Costs

The initial investment for an ATM business includes:

- New ATM machine: $2,000-$8,000 (depending on features)
- Used ATM machine: $1,000-$4,000
- Cash to stock the machine: $1,000-$10,000 (depending on location)
- Permits and licenses: $100-$500
- Insurance: $500-$1,000 annually

In total, you might need $5,000-$15,000 to get started with your first ATM, making this a step up from vending machines but still accessible after you've been consistently profitable with your hustle.

Finding Profitable Locations

The best locations for ATMs include:

- Convenience stores
- Nightclubs and bars
- Festivals and events
- Gas stations
- Restaurants (especially those that are cash-only)
- Hotels (smaller, independent ones)

Location agreements typically work in one of two ways:

1. Fixed rent model: You pay the location owner a set monthly amount
2. Revenue share model: You split the transaction fees (typically 50/50 or 60/40)

Your sales skills will be valuable in negotiating these agreements. Focus on the benefits to the location owner: increased foot traffic, longer customer stays, and additional revenue with minimal effort on their part.

Cash Management and Maintenance

ATMs require more attention to security and cash management than vending machines:

- Regular cash replenishment (frequency depends on usage)
- Monitoring transactions remotely
- Maintaining compliance with banking regulations
- Ensuring security of both the machine and your cash transport procedures

You'll need reliable transportation and should consider security measures when servicing your machines.

Scaling the Business

Like vending machines, ATMs scale well:

- One ATM might generate $500-$1,500 in monthly profit
- Three ATMs could bring in $1,500-$4,500 monthly
- Five ATMs could generate $2,500-$7,500 monthly

The key to scaling is reinvesting your profits to purchase additional machines and secure more locations.

Getting Started

To begin an ATM business:

1. Research ATM processors and machine manufacturers
2. Understand your local regulations regarding ATM operations
3. Develop relationships with location owners in high-traffic areas
4. Create a cash management system for loading and monitoring your machines
5. Consider partnering with someone experienced in the industry for your first machine
6. Start with one location, perfect your operation, then expand

ATMs require more capital and have more complexity than vending machines, but they also typically generate higher returns per machine.

AIRBNB ARBITRAGE: RENT AND RELIST

Airbnb arbitrage takes advantage of the difference between long-term rental prices and short-term vacation rental rates. The concept is straightforward: rent a property long-term, then rent it out on Airbnb for more than your costs.

How Airbnb Arbitrage Works

The model works like this:

1. You rent an apartment or house with a standard lease (getting permission from the landlord to sublet)
2. You furnish and prepare the space for short-term guests
3. You list the property on Airbnb at a nightly rate higher than your daily cost
4. Guests book the property, and you pocket the difference between what they pay and what you pay

For example, if you rent an apartment for $1,200 monthly ($40/day) and rent it on Airbnb for an average of $100/night with 50% occupancy, you'd earn approximately $1,500 monthly in revenue, minus your rent and expenses.

Startup Costs

To get started with Airbnb arbitrage, you'll need:

- Security deposit and first month's rent: $2,000-$4,000
- Furniture and decor: $2,000-$5,000
- Linens, towels, and supplies: $500-$1,000
- Professional cleaning: $200-$500
- Photography: $200-$400
- Licenses and permits: Varies by location

Your total initial investment might be $5,000-$10,000 per property, making this more capital-intensive than vending machines but potentially more profitable.

Finding the Right Properties

Success in Airbnb arbitrage depends on choosing the right properties:

- Look for areas with high tourist or business traveler traffic
- Research local regulations regarding short-term rentals
- Focus on properties with amenities guests value (good location, parking, etc.)
- Calculate all costs carefully to ensure profitability
- Consider seasonal fluctuations in demand

The key is finding properties where the gap between long-term and short-term rental rates is substantial enough to create profit after all expenses.

Getting Landlord Approval

This is where your hustle skills really matter. Many landlords initially reject the idea of their property being used for Airbnb. Here's how to approach them:

- Be completely transparent about your intentions
- Offer additional security deposit or slightly higher rent
- Present a detailed business plan showing how you'll manage the property
- Propose a profit-sharing arrangement
- Address concerns about insurance, property care, and tenant screening

Remember, you're essentially selling the landlord on a business partnership. Approach it with the same preparation and professionalism you would any important sale.

Managing the Property

The ongoing work involved includes:

- Communicating with guests before and during their stay
- Coordinating cleaning between guests
- Maintaining the property and addressing any issues
- Managing bookings and calendar availability
- Optimizing your listing to maintain high occupancy

While more time-intensive than vending machines or ATMs, much of this can be systematized or outsourced as you scale.

Scaling the Business

Airbnb arbitrage scales by adding more properties:

- One property might net $500-$1,500 monthly
- Three properties could generate $1,500-$4,500 monthly
- Five properties could bring in $2,500-$7,500 monthly

With each property you add, your systems become more efficient, and your profit margins can improve.

Getting Started

To begin with Airbnb arbitrage:

1. Research your local market to understand demand, pricing, and regulations

2. Calculate potential profits based on realistic occupancy rates and expenses
3. Prepare a professional presentation for potential landlords
4. Start with one property in a proven location
5. Create systems for guest communication, cleaning, and management
6. Reinvest profits to secure additional properties

This model requires more active management than vending or ATM machines, but also offers higher potential returns and scalability.

AFFILIATE MARKETING: ONLINE CONSIGNMENT FOR THE DIGITAL AGE

Affiliate marketing is essentially digital consignment—you promote other people's products and get paid a commission when someone buys through your recommendation. It's a natural extension of hustling skills into the online world.

How Affiliate Marketing Works

The basic model is:

1. You join affiliate programs for products you believe in
2. You promote these products through various channels (social media, website, email)
3. You include special tracking links in your promotions
4. When someone clicks your link and makes a purchase, you earn a commission
5. The company handles products, shipping, and customer service

Commissions typically range from 5% to 50% depending on the product type. Digital products like courses and software often offer the highest commission rates.

Startup Costs

One of the most attractive aspects of affiliate marketing is the low startup cost:

- Website domain and hosting: $100-$200 annually
- Content creation tools: $0-$500
- Email marketing platform: $0-$30 monthly
- Social media scheduling tools: $0-$50 monthly

With as little as $300, you can set up a basic affiliate marketing operation, making this one of the most accessible passive income strategies for new hustlers.

Choosing Products to Promote

The key to ethical and effective affiliate marketing is promoting products you genuinely believe in:

- Products you've personally used and benefited from
- Items that solve real problems for your audience
- High-quality offerings with good customer support
- Products with competitive commission rates and tracking
- Items relevant to your personal brand or story

Your hustle experience gives you insight into what makes a product worth promoting—the same principles of value and authenticity apply online.

Building Your Promotion Channels

Unlike physical products that you sell in person, affiliate marketing requires digital distribution channels:

- **Social Media:** Build authentic followings on platforms where your target audience spends time
- **YouTube:** Create review videos, tutorials, or demonstration content
- **Blog/Website:** Write helpful content that naturally incorporates product recommendations
- **Email List:** Build a subscriber base you can regularly share recommendations with
- **Digital Products:** Create guides or resources that include affiliate recommendations

Each channel has different strengths, but all require building trust with your audience before promoting products.

The Connection to Street Consignment

In my interview, I mentioned how affiliate marketing is like a legal version of street consignment. The parallels are clear:

- Instead of taking physical products to sell, you're taking digital links

- Rather than splitting profits on the street, commissions are tracked and paid automatically
- The supplier (company) handles inventory and fulfillment, just like in traditional consignment
- Your reputation and trust with your audience determine your success

The difference is that affiliate marketing is completely legal, has unlimited scale potential, and doesn't require you to carry inventory or handle cash transactions.

Getting Started

To begin with affiliate marketing:

1. Identify products relevant to your personal brand or story
2. Join affiliate programs for those products (Amazon Associates is an easy starting point)
3. Create content that genuinely helps people and naturally incorporates your affiliate products
4. Focus on building trust first, sales second
5. Track which promotions work best and double down on successful approaches
6. Reinvest early earnings into better content creation and distribution

Start small, be authentic, and focus on providing real value—the commissions will follow.

DIGITAL PRODUCTS: CREATE ONCE, SELL FOREVER

Creating and selling your own digital products might be the ultimate passive income strategy. Once created, digital products can be sold infinitely with virtually no additional costs.

Types of Digital Products You Can Create

Based on your hustling experience, you could create various digital products:

- **E-books:** Share your sales techniques, motivation strategies, or business systems
- **Online Courses:** Teach others how to start their own hustle or scale an existing one
- **Templates:** Create business plans, sales scripts, or system documents others can use
- **Apps or Software:** Develop tools that solve problems for other entrepreneurs
- **Membership Sites:** Build a community where you share ongoing advice and resources

As someone who's been successful with street sales and is now building a book, you're already on the path to creating valuable digital products.

Startup Costs

Creating digital products requires minimal financial investment:

- Design software or services: $0-$500
- Hosting and sales platform: $0-$50 monthly
- Marketing materials: $0-$300
- Optional professional services (editing, design): $200-$1,000

With $500-$1,000, you could create your first professional digital product, making this accessible after a few months of successful hustling.

Creating Your First Digital Product

The process of creating a digital product typically includes:

1. **Identify a Specific Problem:** What struggle do people in your target audience face?
2. **Develop a Solution:** How can your knowledge help solve this problem?
3. **Create the Content:** Write, record, or design your product
4. **Package It Professionally:** Ensure it looks polished and valuable
5. **Set Up Sales Systems:** Choose platforms to sell and deliver your product
6. **Launch and Promote:** Get your product in front of potential buyers

Your first product doesn't need to be perfect—it just needs to provide genuine value to buyers.

Selling Without Being "Salesy"

The key to selling digital products is the same as successful street hustling:

- Focus on the transformation your product provides, not just its features
- Share authentic stories of how your knowledge has helped you or others
- Be transparent about what buyers will and won't get
- Offer a satisfaction guarantee to reduce purchase risk
- Let your genuine belief in your product shine through

The same confidence and authenticity that helps you sell hats on the street will help you sell digital products online.

Scaling Your Digital Product Business

Once you have one successful digital product, scaling becomes easier:

- Create complementary products that solve related problems
- Develop different formats of the same content (turn an e-book into a course)
- Increase your promotional efforts to reach larger audiences
- Raise prices as you build a reputation for quality
- Implement affiliate programs so others promote your products

Unlike physical products, digital products have nearly infinite profit margins after covering your initial creation costs.

Getting Started

To begin creating digital products:

1. List your areas of expertise based on your hustling experience

2. Identify specific problems you can help others solve
3. Outline your first product (start small—maybe a guide or template)
4. Set aside dedicated time to create your product
5. Research platforms for selling (Gumroad, Teachable, or your own website)
6. Create a simple launch plan to promote your product

Remember that your first product is just the beginning. Each product you create builds on your reputation and adds another passive income stream to your portfolio.

CREATING YOUR PASSIVE INCOME PORTFOLIO

Now that we've covered several passive income opportunities, let's talk about how to build a balanced portfolio that works for you.

Start with One, Master It, Then Expand

Don't try to pursue all these opportunities at once. Instead:

1. Choose ONE passive income stream that aligns best with your interests, capital, and skills
2. Invest the time to truly understand that business model
3. Get it profitable and systematized
4. Only then, add your second passive income stream

This focused approach prevents the common mistake of spreading yourself too thin across multiple half-started ventures.

Balance Your Time and Money Investments

Different passive income streams require different combinations of time and money:

- Vending/ATM machines: Higher money investment, lower time investment
- Airbnb arbitrage: Medium money investment, higher time investment
- Affiliate marketing: Lower money investment, medium time investment
- Digital products: Lower money investment, higher initial time investment

Choose opportunities that match your current resources. If you have more time than money, start with affiliate marketing or digital products. If you've saved up from your hustle, vending machines or ATMs might be better options.

Create Complementary Income Streams

As you add multiple income streams, look for complementary relationships:

- Your social media presence for hat sales can also support affiliate marketing
- Your experience managing vending machines provides skills for ATM operations
- Customer service systems for Airbnb can translate to digital product support

Each business should make the others stronger, not compete for the same resources.

Track Performance and Double Down on Winners

Not every passive income stream will perform equally well for you. Implement tracking systems to monitor:

- Total revenue
- Profit margin
- Time investment
- Growth potential
- Stability/consistency

Focus your expansion efforts on the streams that deliver the best overall results, not just the highest immediate returns.

ACTION STEPS:

1. **Passive Income Research:** Choose the two opportunities from this chapter that interest you most. For each one, find three people who are successfully doing it and study their approach (through social media, YouTube, or direct outreach).
2. **Capital Planning:** Calculate how much startup capital you need for your chosen opportunity. Create a specific savings plan to reach that amount within a realistic timeframe.
3. **Skills Assessment:** List the specific skills required for your chosen passive income stream. Rate yourself on each skill and identify areas where you need to improve or learn.

4. **Local Market Analysis:** For location-based opportunities (vending, ATMs, Airbnb), identify 5-10 potential locations in your area and assess their potential based on foot traffic, competition, and accessibility.

5. **First Step Commitment:** Choose ONE passive income opportunity and commit to completing a specific first step within the next week (such as contacting a vending machine supplier, registering for an affiliate program, or outlining a digital product).

Remember, the transition from active hustling to passive income isn't overnight—it's a gradual process of building assets that work for you. The street hustle teaches you to work hard for money; passive income teaches you to make money work hard for you.

The streets may have taught us how to grind, but passive income teaches us how to build wealth that lasts for generations.

CHAPTER 9

STAY SHARP, STAY LEGAL

THE DANGERS OF FAST MONEY
VS. SMART MONEY

Let's have a real conversation about something I've seen firsthand: the difference between fast money and smart money.

Fast money is tempting. You see it around you—people selling drugs, running scams, or hustling in ways that cross legal lines. These people might flash cash, wear expensive clothes, and seem like they've got it all figured out. I know because I've been tempted by that path myself.

When I was younger, I sold weed. I thought I was on my way to making it. Then one day, after an incident at school, I ended up in a situation where people shot at the car I was in. Four bullets hit my door, but didn't go through. That was God protecting me, showing me I needed to choose a different path.

Fast money comes with costs that don't show up on Instagram:

- The constant fear of getting caught
- The risk of violence from competitors or customers

- The damage to your family and community
- The criminal record that follows you forever
- The limited ceiling on how far you can go

Smart money takes longer to build, but it compounds over time without those dangers. It might not give you a Rolex next week, but it can give you real freedom for the rest of your life.

Think about it this way: Fast money is a sprint that usually ends in a crash. Smart money is a marathon that ends with you crossing a finish line that many people never even see.

WHY STAYING LEGAL IS LONG-TERM WEALTH INSURANCE

When you choose legal hustles, you're buying insurance for your future wealth. Here's what I mean:

Protection from Loss

When you operate legally:

- Your assets can't be seized by law enforcement
- Your business can't be shut down overnight
- Your money can be kept in banks where it's safe and can grow
- Your income can be explained and documented

I've seen people lose everything they built because it wasn't built on legal ground. All those years of hustling, gone in a single day.

Access to Opportunities

Legal business opens doors that remain closed to illegal operators:

- Bank loans to expand your business
- Rental agreements for prime locations
- Partnerships with established companies
- Investment opportunities that require background checks
- Government contracts and grants

Every dollar you make legally can be leveraged to make more dollars. Illegal money hits a ceiling quickly.

Peace of Mind

The value of peace of mind can't be overstated:

- Sleeping without worrying about raids or arrests
- Walking in public without looking over your shoulder
- Interacting with police without anxiety
- Planning for the future with confidence
- Being honest with your family about your work

I sleep better knowing that my hustle is something I can be proud of, something I can talk about openly, something that builds up my community instead of tearing it down.

Legacy Building

Legal businesses can be passed down to future generations:

- You can teach your children how to operate the business
- You can sell the business when you're ready to move on
- You can donate to causes you care about
- You can inspire others to follow a positive path
- You can break generational curses instead of reinforcing them

Remember what I said about nobody in my family ever being a millionaire or financially free? I want to change that pattern, and I can only do it by building something legal and lasting.

BUILDING CREDIT: YOUR FINANCIAL REPUTATION

In the streets, your reputation is everything. In the financial world, your credit score is your reputation. Building good credit is essential for long-term wealth creation.

Why Credit Matters

A strong credit score gives you access to:

- Lower interest rates on loans
- Better terms on credit cards
- Approval for apartment rentals
- Lower insurance premiums
- Job opportunities (some employers check credit)

Without good credit, you'll pay more for everything and be denied opportunities that could accelerate your wealth building.

Getting Started with Credit

If you're young or have no credit history:

1. **Start with a secured credit card:** Put down a deposit (often $200-$500) that becomes your credit limit.
2. **Become an authorized user:** If someone you trust has good credit, ask to be added to their account.
3. **Get a credit-builder loan:** Some credit unions offer these specifically to help establish credit.
4. **Use a co-signer:** For your first loan, having someone co-sign can help you get approved.

Building Strong Credit

Once you have credit, follow these principles:

- **Pay on time, every time:** Payment history is the most import-ant factor in your credit score.
- **Keep utilization low:** Try to use less than 30% of your avail-able credit.
- **Don't close old accounts:** Length of credit history matters.
- **Limit new applications:** Only apply for credit you truly need.
- **Monitor your credit report:** Check annually for errors or fraud.

Rebuilding Bad Credit

If you've made mistakes in the past:

- **Start paying on time now:** Recent history counts more than old problems.
- **Negotiate with creditors:** Sometimes you can arrange payment plans or settlements.
- **Use secured credit products:** Rebuild trust with secured cards or loans.
- **Be patient:** Negative items generally fall off your report after 7 years.

Your credit score isn't just a number—it's a tool that can either accelerate or hinder your wealth-building journey. Treat it with the same care you'd treat your reputation on the streets.

REGISTERING YOUR BUSINESS: MAKING IT OFFICIAL

When I first started selling hats, I was just a guy with products. Now I'm working toward building a legitimate business. Here's why registering your business matters and how to do it.

Benefits of Business Registration

Operating as a registered business provides:

- **Legal protection:** Separating personal and business liability
- **Tax advantages:** Access to business deductions and tax structures

- **Credibility:** Looking professional to customers and partners
- **Growth opportunities:** Ability to raise capital, sign contracts, and scale
- **Wealth building:** Creating an asset that can be sold or passed down

Types of Business Structures

There are several ways to structure your business:

Sole Proprietorship:

- Easiest to set up (you might already be one without knowing it)
- No separation between you and the business
- All profits pass directly to your personal taxes
- You're personally liable for all business debts and legal issues

Limited Liability Company (LLC):

- Provides personal liability protection
- Relatively simple and inexpensive to set up
- Flexible tax options
- Can have multiple owners (members)
- Good option for most small businesses

Corporation (S-Corp or C-Corp):

- Strongest legal protection
- More complex structure with shareholders, directors, and officers
- Potentially significant tax advantages at higher income levels

- More paperwork and compliance requirements
- Better for raising outside investment

For most hustlers starting out, an LLC provides the best balance of protection, simplicity, and flexibility.

How to Register Your Business

The process varies by state, but generally includes:

1. **Choose a business name:** Make sure it's available and distinctive
2. **Select a business structure:** Usually an LLC for new entrepreneurs
3. **File formation documents:** Submit articles of organization to your state
4. **Get an EIN:** Employer Identification Number from the IRS
5. **Open a business bank account:** Keep personal and business finances separate
6. **Obtain necessary licenses:** Research requirements for your specific business
7. **Register for taxes:** Sales tax, income tax, and any industry-specific taxes

Many of these steps can be completed online, and the total cost is typically $100-$500 depending on your state and business type.

When to Register

You don't need to register your business on day one of your hustle. Consider registration when:

- You're consistently making profit
- You're ready to separate personal and business finances
- You want to sign formal agreements with suppliers or customers
- You're concerned about potential liability
- You're planning to scale beyond just yourself

The right time to register is when the benefits outweigh the costs and administrative requirements.

KEEPING CLEAN BOOKS: TRACKING YOUR MONEY

Clean bookkeeping isn't just for big corporations—it's essential for any serious entrepreneur. Here's why it matters and how to do it right.

Why Good Bookkeeping Matters

Proper financial records allow you to:

- Know exactly how profitable your business really is
- Make informed decisions about pricing and expenses
- Prepare accurate tax returns and maximize deductions
- Secure financing when you need to grow
- Identify theft, waste, or inefficiencies

Without clean books, you're essentially hustling blindfolded.

Basic Bookkeeping Systems

You don't need anything fancy to start. Begin with:

1. **Separate accounts:** Keep personal and business money completely separate
2. **Income tracking:** Record every sale with date, amount, and source
3. **Expense tracking:** Save receipts and record all business expenses
4. **Regular reconciliation:** Compare your records to bank statements monthly
5. **Profit calculation:** Calculate revenue minus expenses at least monthly

You can start with a simple spreadsheet or even a notebook. As you grow, consider apps like Wave (free) or QuickBooks (paid but more powerful).

Important Financial Records to Keep

At minimum, maintain:

- **Sales receipts:** Records of all income
- **Expense receipts:** Proof of all business purchases
- **Bank statements:** Monthly records from your business accounts
- **Tax documents:** Any forms related to your business taxes

- **Contracts and agreements:** Documentation of all business relationships

Keep these records for at least seven years to be safe for tax purposes.

Common Bookkeeping Mistakes to Avoid

Don't fall into these traps:

- **Mixing personal and business money:** This creates tax problems and confusion
- **Waiting until tax time:** Update your books weekly or at least monthly
- **Losing receipts:** They're your proof for tax deductions
- **Not tracking cash sales:** Every dollar needs to be recorded
- **Doing it all yourself:** As you grow, consider hiring a bookkeeper

Clean books might not seem exciting, but they're the foundation of a business that can grow beyond the hustle stage.

TAXES: PAYING YOUR SHARE WITHOUT OVERPAYING

Many hustlers operate in cash and avoid taxes altogether. While that might seem advantageous in the short term, it creates significant long-term problems. Here's how to handle taxes properly without paying more than you should.

Understanding Self-Employment Taxes

When you work for yourself, you're responsible for:

- **Income tax:** Federal, state, and sometimes local
- **Self-employment tax:** Both the employer and employee portions of Social Security and Medicare (currently 15.3%)

This means setting aside approximately 25-30% of your profit for taxes, depending on your income level and state.

Tax Deductions for Hustlers

The good news is that business expenses reduce your taxable income. Common deductions include:

- **Inventory costs:** What you pay for products you resell
- **Business supplies:** Materials needed to operate your business
- **Travel expenses:** Mileage driving to selling locations or suppliers
- **Phone and internet:** The portion used for business
- **Home office:** If you have a dedicated space for business
- **Education:** Books, courses, or coaching related to your business
- **Insurance:** Any business-related coverage
- **Legal and professional fees:** Costs for lawyers, accountants, or consultants

Keeping detailed records of these expenses is crucial for claiming deductions properly.

Quarterly Estimated Taxes

Unlike employees who have taxes withheld from each paycheck, self-employed individuals need to:

1. Estimate their annual tax liability
2. Pay this amount in quarterly installments (April 15, June 15, September 15, January 15)
3. File an annual tax return reconciling these payments

Failing to make quarterly payments can result in penalties and interest.

Working with Tax Professionals

As your business grows, consider working with:

- **Tax preparers:** Help file correct returns
- **Enrolled agents:** Tax specialists who can represent you before the IRS
- **CPAs:** Provide more comprehensive tax planning and strategy

The cost of professional help is often offset by the tax savings they identify and the peace of mind they provide.

Tax Strategies for Growth

As your income increases, explore more advanced strategies:

- **Business entity optimization:** Choosing the right structure for tax efficiency

- **Retirement accounts:** SEP IRAs, Solo 401(k)s, and other tax-advantaged options
- **Timing of income and expenses:** Strategic decisions about when to receive income or make purchases
- **Health insurance deductions:** Options for self-employed health care costs

These strategies can significantly reduce your tax burden while keeping you fully compliant with tax laws.

INSURANCE: PROTECTING WHAT YOU BUILD

As you grow your wealth and business, protecting them becomes increasingly important. Here's why insurance matters and what types to consider.

Types of Insurance for Entrepreneurs

Depending on your specific hustle, consider:

General Liability Insurance:

- Protects against claims of bodily injury or property damage
- Essential for businesses with physical locations or customer interactions
- Typically costs $500-$1,500 annually for small businesses

Professional Liability Insurance:

- Covers claims of mistakes, negligence, or failure to perform
- Important for service-based businesses

- Usually ranges from $500-$2,000 annually

Property Insurance:

- Protects business equipment, inventory, and locations
- Necessary if you have significant physical assets
- Cost varies based on value of property insured

Business Interruption Insurance:

- Provides income if your business can't operate due to disaster
- Important if your income depends on specific locations or equipment
- Often bundled with property insurance

Health Insurance:

- Critical for your personal well-being and financial security
- Options include Marketplace plans, association health plans, or health sharing ministries
- Costs vary widely based on coverage and location

Life Insurance:

- Protects your family and business partners if something happens to you
- Term life insurance is affordable for young entrepreneurs
- Can also be used as an investment vehicle (whole life or IUL policies)

In our interview, I mentioned investing in an IUL (Indexed Universal Life) policy. These combine life insurance with a cash value component that can grow tax-advantaged, providing both protection and investment potential.

When to Get Insured

For most hustlers, insurance becomes important when:

- You have valuable business assets to protect
- You interact with customers who could potentially sue
- You have family members who depend on your income
- Your business has grown beyond what you could easily restart
- You're operating in higher-risk environments or industries

Don't wait until you "make it big" to get basic coverage. The time to get insured is before you need it.

PLANNING FOR THE NEXT LEVEL

As your hustle grows and you build passive income streams, it's time to think about next-level wealth building. Here are strategies to consider as you advance.

Real Estate Investment

Beyond Airbnb arbitrage, consider:

- **Rental properties:** Buy properties that generate monthly cash flow
- **House hacking:** Live in one unit of a multi-unit property while renting others

- **Commercial real estate:** Invest in retail, office, or industrial properties
- **REITs:** Real Estate Investment Trusts for passive exposure to property markets

Real estate has created more millionaires than perhaps any other investment vehicle.

Business Expansion and Diversification

Look for opportunities to:

- **Add complementary products or services:** Expand what you offer current customers
- **Enter new markets:** Take your successful model to different locations or demographics
- **Acquire related businesses:** Buy existing operations instead of building from scratch
- **Create franchise systems:** Package your business model for others to implement

Expansion multiplies your income without requiring proportional increases in your time.

Building Your Network

As you grow, your network becomes increasingly valuable:

- **Find mentors:** Connect with those who have achieved what you're aiming for

- **Join masterminds:** Groups of like-minded entrepreneurs who share insights
- **Attend industry events:** Build relationships with suppliers, partners, and customers
- **Create strategic alliances:** Partner with complementary businesses

Remember how I mentioned meeting Neo and being invited to a seven-figure mastermind? That connection multiplied my opportunities overnight. Your network truly determines your net worth.

Continued Education and Growth

Never stop learning:

- **Formal education:** Consider degrees or certifications if they add specific value
- **Self-education:** Books, courses, and mentorship in business and investing
- **Skill development:** Continue building capabilities that increase your value
- **Mindset work:** Develop the psychology of wealth and success

The more you learn, the more you earn—and the more effectively you can manage and grow what you earn.

ACTION STEPS:

1. **Legal Hustle Audit:** Review all aspects of your current hustle and ensure everything is operating within legal boundaries. Identify any areas that need adjustment to be fully compliant.

2. **Credit Check:** Get a free copy of your credit report from AnnualCreditReport.com and review it for accuracy. If you don't have established credit yet, take one specific step toward building it this month.

3. **Business Structure Research:** Research the requirements for forming an LLC in your state. Create a timeline for when registration makes sense based on your current business progress.

4. **Bookkeeping System Setup:** Establish a simple but consistent system for tracking all business income and expenses. If you already have one, review it for completeness and accuracy.

5. **Insurance Evaluation:** Make a list of potential risks in your business and research appropriate insurance coverage. Get at least one quote for general liability insurance to understand the cost.

Remember: Staying legal isn't just about avoiding problems—it's about creating possibilities. Every step you take to legitimize and protect your hustle opens new doors for growth and opportunity.

The streets may have taught us how to make money, but staying sharp and legal teaches us how to build wealth that lasts for generations.

CHAPTER 10

THE FUTURE CEO

WHERE I'M HEADED NEXT

When my grandmother looked me in my eyes before she passed in July 2023, she said two things that changed my life: "Boy, you gonna be on that stage," and "You the man of the house now." In that moment, she passed me both a blessing and a responsibility.

I took that seriously. At 17, I stepped up. I started selling hats when my mom needed rent money. I chose the legal path when the illegal one was right in front of me. I began building something real when most people my age were just thinking about the weekend.

But this is just the beginning.

Where am I headed next? Let me share my vision with you:

Building a Brand, Not Just a Business My "Without God I'm Nothing" hats are just the starting point. I'm working to build this into a recognizable brand that stands for faith, hustle, and positive impact. I see clothing lines, accessories, and products that carry this message to people everywhere.

Expanding from Products to Platform I'm moving beyond just selling physical products to creating a platform where I can share my message and help others. This book is part of that vision—taking what I've learned and using it to lift others up. I see speaking engagements, courses, and mentorship programs in my future.

Investing in Real Assets As my hustle generates more capital, I'm strategically investing in assets that create passive income. Vending machines, ATMs, real estate—these aren't just dreams, they're plans in motion. My goal is to have multiple streams of income that work for me 24/7.

Creating Opportunities for Others Success means nothing if I can't bring others with me. I'm building systems to create opportunities for people in my community—whether that's through my business, through teaching them what I've learned, or through investing in their visions.

The 17-year-old selling hats in parking lots is becoming something bigger: a CEO with a vision that extends far beyond making daily sales. I'm building a legacy.

USING YOUR STORY TO INSPIRE OTHERS

One of the most powerful assets you have isn't in your bank account—it's your story. Your journey, with all its struggles and triumphs, has the power to inspire others and open doors you never imagined.

The Power of Personal Narrative

Your story matters because:

- It creates authentic connection with others
- It demonstrates what's possible to those still struggling
- It establishes your credibility in a way credentials can't
- It attracts opportunities and relationships aligned with your purpose
- It gives meaning to your hustle beyond just making money

My story of paying my mom's rent when we were three months behind, choosing legal hustle after getting shot at, and connecting with successful entrepreneurs like Neo and Ash—these experiences aren't just things that happened to me. They're parts of a narrative that inspires others and creates opportunities.

How to Share Your Story Effectively

Sharing your story isn't about bragging—it's about connecting and inspiring. Here's how to do it effectively:

Be Authentic Share both struggles and successes. People connect with real experiences, not perfect ones. When I tell people about making $800 a day now, I also tell them about starting with just enough money to buy a few hats.

Focus on Transformation Highlight not just what happened, but how it changed you. When I talk about getting shot at, I emphasize how that moment transformed my understanding of what really matters.

Connect to Universal Themes Link your personal experience to themes others can relate to: family responsibility, choosing right over easy, faith during difficulty, or perseverance through rejection.

Share Purposefully Know why you're telling your story. Is it to inspire? To teach? To connect? Your purpose shapes how and what you share.

Adapt to Your Audience The core of your story stays the same, but how you tell it might change based on who's listening. I might emphasize different aspects when talking to teenagers versus business investors.

Platforms for Sharing Your Story

As you grow, look for platforms to share your journey:

- **Social media** creates your own direct channel to audiences
- **Speaking engagements** at schools, churches, or community organizations
- **Interviews** on podcasts, local media, or online shows
- **Mentorship relationships** where your experience guides others
- **Your products and brand** which can embody elements of your story

My "Without God I'm Nothing" hats aren't just products—they're physical reminders of my story and values. Each sale isn't just a transaction; it's sharing a piece of my journey with someone else.

LEAVING A LEGACY WHILE YOU LIVE

Legacy isn't something that begins after you're gone—it's something you build while you're here. The decisions you make today create ripples that extend far beyond your lifetime.

Breaking Generational Curses

True legacy often begins with breaking negative cycles:

- Financial struggles and poverty mindsets
- Limited education and opportunity
- Destructive habits and lifestyles
- Negative beliefs about what's possible

When I say nobody in my family has ever been a millionaire or financially free, I'm not just stating a fact—I'm identifying a cycle I'm committed to breaking. My success isn't just for me; it's for those who come after me.

Building Generational Wealth

Beyond just accumulating money, generational wealth includes:

- **Financial assets** that can be passed down
- **Knowledge and skills** that create lasting advantage
- **Networks and relationships** that open doors for your family
- **Values and principles** that guide smart decisions
- **Legal structures** (trusts, LLCs, etc.) that protect what you build

The systems and investments we've discussed throughout this book aren't just about making you money now—they're about creating resources that can benefit your children and grandchildren.

Impact Beyond Family

True legacy extends beyond blood relations to community impact:

- **Job creation** through your business growth
- **Mentorship** of young people facing similar challenges
- **Community investment** in the places that shaped you
- **Philanthropy** directed toward causes you care about
- **Inspiration** that changes how others see what's possible

Every time I convince a young person to hustle legally instead of taking dangerous shortcuts, that's legacy in action. Every time I show someone from my neighborhood that entrepreneurship is a viable path, that's legacy in action.

Living Your Legacy Now

Don't wait to start building your legacy:

1. **Define your core values:** What principles do you want to be remembered for?
2. **Make aligned decisions:** Let those values guide your daily choices.
3. **Document your journey:** Keep records of your growth and lessons learned.
4. **Teach what you learn:** Share knowledge as you acquire it.

5. **Build with permanence in mind:** Create systems and assets designed to outlast you.

When my grandmother told me I'd be on stage someday, she was seeing something in me that I hadn't yet seen in myself. Now, I'm not just working to fulfill her vision—I'm expanding it into something that will echo long after both of us are gone.

BALANCING GROWTH AND GROUNDEDNESS

As you achieve more success, one of the biggest challenges becomes staying grounded. I've already had a taste of this from being in rooms with successful people wearing quarter-million-dollar watches, saying that's "something slight." It would be easy to get caught up in that world and lose what made you special in the first place.

Signs of Losing Groundedness

Watch for these warning signs as you grow:

- Disconnecting from the community that supported you
- Focusing on status symbols rather than meaningful impact
- Becoming less accessible to those who need your guidance
- Forgetting the struggles that shaped your character
- Prioritizing appearance of success over actual value creation

Strategies to Stay Grounded

Here's how I plan to maintain my groundedness as I grow:

Remember Where You Came From Regularly revisit the places and connect with the people who knew you before success. This keeps your journey in perspective and your priorities clear.

Maintain Spiritual Foundation For me, my relationship with God is my anchor. Without this spiritual grounding, success could easily become about ego rather than purpose. As my hats say, "Without God I'm Nothing."

Practice Gratitude Daily Acknowledge that your success isn't solely your own doing. Express thanks for the opportunities, support, and even challenges that have shaped your path.

Keep Learning and Growing The moment you think you know everything is the moment you stop growing. Maintain the mindset of a student, regardless of your achievements.

Give Back Meaningfully Find ways to give back that go beyond just writing checks. Invest your time, knowledge, and presence in ways that create real impact.

Surround Yourself with Truth-Tellers Keep people in your life who will tell you the truth, not just what you want to hear. These relationships are invaluable as you navigate increasing success.

Measure Success Beyond Money Develop personal metrics for success that include impact, growth, relationships, and fulfillment—not just financial achievements.

The most respected leaders aren't just those who achieve great things, but those who remain accessible, humble, and grounded despite their achievements.

THE LEADER YOU'RE BECOMING

Leadership isn't just about what you accomplish—it's about who you become in the process. As your hustle grows into a business and your business grows into an enterprise, your personal development as a leader becomes increasingly important.

The Evolution from Hustler to Leader

This evolution typically follows a path:

1. **Solo Hustler:** Doing everything yourself, focused on daily survival
2. **Team Builder:** Learning to work with and through others
3. **System Creator:** Developing processes that scale beyond your direct efforts
4. **Vision Carrier:** Inspiring others toward a larger purpose
5. **Legacy Builder:** Creating impact that outlasts your direct involvement

Each stage requires new skills, perspectives, and priorities. The hustle skills that got you started remain valuable, but they must be supplemented by leadership capabilities.

Leadership Qualities to Develop

As I continue my journey, here are the leadership qualities I'm working to strengthen:

Vision and Communication The ability to see possibilities others don't see yet, and communicate those possibilities in ways that inspire action. This means getting comfortable speaking to groups, crafting compelling messages, and painting a picture of the future that others want to be part of.

Decision-Making Under Uncertainty As a leader, you'll never have perfect information, but you'll still need to make decisions that others will follow. This requires developing good judgment, trusting your instincts, and taking calculated risks.

Building and Empowering Teams No great vision is achieved alone. Leadership means finding the right people, putting them in the right roles, and giving them the tools and authority to succeed. This requires letting go of control while maintaining accountability.

Adaptability and Resilience The business landscape constantly changes. Leaders must be able to adapt strategies while staying true to core principles, and bounce back from setbacks without losing momentum.

Ethical Decision-Making As your influence grows, so does your responsibility. Leaders face situations where the right choice isn't always the easy or profitable one. Developing a strong ethical foundation guides these decisions.

Continuous Self-Development The best leaders never stop growing. They read extensively, seek mentorship, reflect on their experiences, and continuously sharpen their skills.

I'm committed to developing these qualities not just to grow my business, but to grow into the leader I need to become to fulfill my grandmother's vision of me "on that stage"—impacting lives far beyond what I could accomplish through hustle alone.

A FINAL MESSAGE TO YOUNG ENTREPRENEURS

If you're reading this and you're young—whether you're 17 like I was when I started, or 25 and feeling like you're starting late—I want to leave you with some final thoughts.

Your Age is an Advantage, Not a Limitation

Being young gives you:

- Time to fail, learn, and try again
- Energy to hustle harder than most
- Fresh perspective that can disrupt industries
- Technological fluency older entrepreneurs may lack
- The ability to take risks before major responsibilities

Don't wait until you have more experience or resources. Start now, with what you have, where you are.

Choose Your Path Intentionally

Every day, you're making choices that shape your future:

- Between quick money and sustainable wealth
- Between isolation and strategic relationships

- Between consumption and investment
- Between copying others and developing your unique value

These choices might seem small in the moment, but they compound over time to create dramatically different outcomes.

Find Your "Why" Beyond Money

Money is a powerful motivator, but it's not enough to sustain you through the hardest challenges. Dig deeper:

- Who are you doing this for?
- What change do you want to create?
- What legacy do you want to leave?
- What would make you proud looking back 20 years from now?

My "why" started with helping my mom make rent, but it grew into breaking generational curses and creating opportunities for others. Your "why" will evolve too, but you need to start with something meaningful.

Embrace Both Hustle and Rest

Grinding is necessary, but sustainable success requires balance:

- Work intensely when it's time to work
- Rest intentionally to recharge
- Celebrate victories along the way
- Build relationships that provide support
- Take care of your physical and mental health

Remember, the goal isn't just to make it—it's to make it and enjoy it, to build something that brings fulfillment along with success.

Start Where You Are, Use What You Have

Don't wait for perfect conditions:

- If you have a product idea but limited capital, start selling hand-to-hand
- If you have knowledge but no platform, start sharing on free social media
- If you have time but no money, invest your hours in learning and relationships
- If you have passion but no experience, volunteer or apprentice to gain skills

Every successful entrepreneur started somewhere, often with far less than they wanted or needed. The difference is they started.

THE STREETS TAUGHT US HOW TO HUSTLE, NOW IT'S TIME TO OWN THE BLOCK

I began this book by sharing how I turned sidewalk sales into a system that generates $800 a day. I showed you the mindset, the sales techniques, the team-building approaches, and the investment strategies that have shaped my journey.

But this book isn't really about selling hats. It's about something much bigger.

It's about taking the hustle, drive, and creativity that many of us learned on the streets and channeling it into something that creates lasting impact. It's about transforming the skills that helped us survive into tools that help us thrive.

The same energy that powers the street economy can build legitimate businesses. The same charisma that makes someone a neighborhood figure can make them a respected CEO. The same strategic thinking that navigates urban challenges can disrupt industries and create opportunities.

The streets taught us how to hustle. Now it's time to own the block—not through intimidation or illegal activities, but through entrepreneurship, investment, and leadership that transforms communities.

My story is still being written, and so is yours. The chapters ahead will be determined by the choices we make today, the values we hold true to, and the vision we pursue with relentless determination.

Whatever your starting point, whatever obstacles you face, know this: You have everything you need to begin. Your background, your struggles, your unique perspective—these aren't disadvantages. They're your edge in a world that needs fresh thinking and authentic leadership.

Start where you are. Use what you have. Do what you can.

The future belongs to those who create it.

—*Businessman Cedric*

www.ingramcontent.com/pod-product-compliance
Lightning Source LLC
Chambersburg PA
CBHW070328130626
46556CB00007B/2774